Make Early Learning Standards Come Alive

Also by Gaye Gronlund:

Focused Early Learning: A Planning Framework for Teaching Young Children

Focused Observations: How to Observe Children for Assessment and Curriculum Planning (with Marlyn James)

Focused Portfolios: A Complete Assessment for the Young Child (with Bev Engel)

Make Early Learning Standards Come Alive

Connecting Your Practice and Curriculum to State Guidelines

Gaye Gronlund

PEARSON

Merrill
Prentice Hall

Upper Saddle River, New Jersey
Columbus, Ohio

Redleaf Press
www.redleafpress.org

This special edition is published by Merrill/Prentice Hall, by arrangement with Redleaf Press, a division of Resources for Child Caring, 10 Yorkton Court, St. Paul, MN 55117.

Vice President and Executive Publisher: Jeffery W. Johnston
Acquisitions Editor: Julie Peters
Director of Marketing: David Gesell
Marketing Manager: Amy Judd
Marketing Coordinator: Brian Mounts

This book was printed and bound by Bind-Rite Graphics. The cover was printed by Phoenix Color Corp.

10 9 8 7 6 5 4 3 2 1
ISBN: 0-13-234036-4

Dedication

To Judith Paiz, Charmaine Espinosa, and Nancy Treat of the New Mexico Office of Child Development: Thank you for giving me the opportunity to learn so much through our work together.

And to all of the early educators in the New Mexico programs who work so hard to meet the standards and document the children's progress.

Acknowledgments

Thanks to Beth Wallace for leading the charge on this book and initiating the ideas and format involved.

And thanks to Eileen Nelson for providing support throughout the editing process. I greatly appreciate it!

Contents

The What and Why of Early Childhood Learning Standards

S tandards, standards everywhere! In the field of early childhood education, standards are the buzz. There are standards that determine the number of children recommended for each teacher in a room. There are standards for the types of learning preschool children should experience. And there

are child outcome standards, standards that define what young children should be learning. This book will focus on the latter: What are the reasonable expectations that guide early educators in planning curriculum for preschool children and in assessing their progress in achieving those expectations?

Early learning standards for preschool children are all around us. As of August 2005, forty-five states had identified standards for communication and literacy, and forty-four had standards for mathematics. In addition, most of these states had developed standards for the areas of science, social studies, social/emotional development, physical development and health, and the creative arts (www.ccsso.org). How can you as

an early childhood educator use these standards in ways that are beneficial to the children? How can you

- implement the standards in a way that is developmentally appropriate and good for the children?

- figure out reasonable and efficient ways to assess the children's progress toward the standards?

- be accountable without testing, without feeling like you are failing children, without feeling overwhelmed by the pressures and expectations of state agencies, political and funding bodies, and the public at large to produce outcomes, to track children's progress, and to increase their success in school?

■ do what's in your heart: taking good care of young children and helping them to grow and learn and flourish?

This book will offer help and hints, support and clarification, and clear explanations of how to make preschool early learning standards come alive in early childhood classrooms and programs. We hope you will find reassurance and direction and feel validated in the work you are already doing with young children. You will be given language and tools to more clearly explain to others just how you are addressing children's learning even though you are doing so by planning for play and exploration, singing and dancing, socialization, and the development of self-help skills.

Ways to assess children's capabilities and progress without testing or pressuring them inappropriately will also be included. Plans for activities and interactions that meet children where they are and help them to move ahead in their development will be outlined. And methods to embrace accountability in a manner that is helpful to you as an early educator and, most important, that is appropriate for young children, will be shared. Outcomes for children that are reasonable and attainable *can* be identified, outcomes that do indeed track their learning and growth.

Facts about Early Learning Standards

Just what are early learning standards for preschool children? The Early Childhood Education Assessment Consortium of the Council of Chief State School Officers (CCSSO) defines early learning standards as follows:

> Statements that describe expectations for the learning and development of young children across the domains of: health and physical well-being; social and emotional well-being; approaches to learning; language development and symbol systems; and general knowledge about the world around them. (www.ccsso.org 2005)

Sometimes the terms used in discussing early learning standards can be confusing. This consortium has developed a glossary of terms on its Web site that is continually updated as new developments occur across the country. In order to help you, we have included more of its definitions related to the language of standards and standards-based assessments in the appendix of this book.

As stated earlier, most U.S. states are developing or have developed some form of standards or identified expectations for children younger than kindergarten age. Most are for the preschool years, ages three to five. Some states have also developed (or are developing) standards or expectations for infants and toddlers. In this book, we will focus on the preschool standards. In many states, the early learning standards have been correlated in some way with elementary and high school educational standards. All have many features in common and are based on generally accepted knowledge of child development. The differences lie in the formatting or the inclusion of specific content or developmental areas. The number of items included in the identified standards also varies widely (from 50 to 371) (Scott-Little, Kagan, and Frelow 2004, 15). On the federal level, Head Start developed a Child Outcomes Framework in 2000. This framework is now an important part of the evaluation of the effectiveness of Head Start programs across the country.

Standards for children younger than kindergarten age differ from those for older children because the primary tasks of young children are to acquire and refine foundational skills— skills that will help them successfully learn the content and information in the later grades. Young children are learning to listen, to work with others, to use their language to express themselves, and to dedicate their attention and energies to specific activities. "In early childhood, the development of these foundational skills (skills that lay the foundation for later learning) is just as important as mastery of content matter" (Shore, Bodrova, and Leong 2004, 5). Therefore, it is recommended that early learning standards include social/emotional development, physical development, and approaches to learning in addition to traditional content areas associated with schooling (Scott-Little, Kagan, and Frelow 2004, 7).

In each state, early learning standards are often given different names. For example, California's early learning standards are called "Desired Results for Children and Families." Those of Indiana are called "The Foundations for Young Children to the Indiana Academic Standards." Montana's are titled "Montana's Early Learning Guidelines," and Connecticut's are called "Connecticut's Preschool Curriculum Framework." But these standards all "describe the same thing—the kinds of development and learning that should be taking place" (Shore, Bodrova, and Leong 2004, 1).

Benefits and Potential Problems of Early Learning Standards

There are many benefits to early learning standards. There are also potential problems and abuses in the ways they are used. First, consider the following benefits:

- They reinforce the fact that there is an incredible potential for learning and growth in the infant, toddler, and preschool years and that there is value and importance in providing quality early childhood programs for children's long-term success in school and in life.

- They help establish expectations for children at different ages and create a commonality for communication about children's accomplishments and capabilities.

- They provide a framework for accountability—a way for early educators to show parents, the community at large, and themselves just what children are learning in early childhood programs.
- Learning standards and developmentally appropriate practices can indeed go together! No change in practices is necessary. Learning standards can be incorporated into play, into emergent curriculum and projects, and into small and large group times. Much of this book will show how to do just that.

In its position statement titled "Early Learning Standards: Creating the Conditions for Success," the National Association for the Education of Young Children (NAEYC) and the National Association of Early Childhood Specialists in State Departments of Education (NAECS/SDE) note: "By defining the desired content and outcomes of young children's education, early learning standards can lead to greater opportunities for positive development and learning in these early years" (NAEYC 2002, 2). And who would not agree that as a society we indeed want greater opportunities for young children? If early learning standards can help us do more to reach this goal, then bring them on!

Throughout the field of education, however, there is cause for concern about how these standards are used. The NAEYC and NAECS/SDE position statement warns that there are educational and developmental risks for vulnerable young children if standards are not well developed and implemented. . . . Thus, a test of the value of any standards effort is whether it promotes positive educational and developmental outcomes and whether it avoids penalizing or excluding children from needed services and supports. (NAEYC 2002, 2)

At a session sponsored by the Massachusetts Department of Education at the 2004 NAEYC Annual Conference, a group of early educators created the following list of pros and cons about the implementation of early learning standards. Read through them and consider what you might add in each category.

Pros to Early Learning Standards

- They can provide richness to our conversations about children's growth and learning.
- We can match standards to what we are already doing.
- They can be linked to primary standards so that we are indeed contributing to school readiness.
- They help us identify next steps and transitions.
- They are a strategy for professionalizing our field.
- They help us communicate across the grades, among ourselves, and with our public.
- They help us to have higher expectations for children.

- They result in authentic assessments tied to standards.
- They provide accountability to us.

Cons to Early Learning Standards

- They lead to teaching to the standards only in a cookie-cutter style curriculum. Then the uniqueness of early childhood education is lost.
- They bring a pressure of accountability with the risk of a push-down in curriculum and inappropriate expectations for younger children.
- Direct instruction is assumed as the only way to guarantee that standards are addressed. The children's learning in self-directed, exploratory ways is not trusted.
- They can contribute to a "we/they" mentality between preschool and elementary teachers.
- They take time for early educators to learn and work through, to figure out how to integrate into good practices. There is a need for reflection and interaction among colleagues in order to do so.
- They can result in testing and other inappropriate assessment methods being used.
- There is little money to support education and training of early educators in the standards and how best to use them.

What else would you add as a pro or con regarding early learning standards?

Making the Best Use of Standards

Yes, early learning standards can be beneficial as well as be misused. How do early educators, then, make the best use of them and still remain true to best practices, to the needs of young children, to the philosophy of Developmentally Appropriate Practice, and to doing what's right for children? There are several important questions to ask when implementing curriculum and assessment related to early learning standards.

1. Are the sources for the expectations of the children age-appropriate, reflective of cultural differences, and flexible in the rate of acquisition of skills and knowledge?

2. How will the children's progress toward the standards and expectations be assessed? Are the methods used based on naturalistic and authentic methods such as observation and portfolio collection rather than on one-time testing?

3. How are early educators trained to learn and understand the standards, to reflect and discuss their depth and breadth, and to plan for learning experiences that are right for young children and still integrate the content of the standards? How are they trained to assess the children's progress toward those standards?

4. How is the information gained in the assessment of progress toward standards used? Is it used to better teach the children and to support their continued growth and develop their potential as learners and constructive members of society? Or is it used to fail children, to deny placements or advancement, to limit their opportunities, or to label them in some way?

The Organization of This Book

This book will focus on the ways to use preschool early learning standards in positive child- and family-friendly ways, integrating them into the best curricular practices of early childhood classrooms. In chapter 2 the focus will be on curriculum: recognizing and planning for ways to make standards come alive in preschool children's play and discovery, in their use of indoor and outdoor environments, in emergent curriculum and projects, and in teacher-led small and large groups. In chapter 3, assessing authentically will be explained. Ways that help you as an early educator better identify children's progress toward standards and use that information to plan more individually and effectively will be shared.

In chapters 4 through 10, standards from a major content area or area of development will be addressed. The areas are as follows: Communication and Literacy, Mathematics, Science, Social Studies, Social/Emotional Development, Physical Devel-opment and Health, and Creative Arts. The information about each specific area is presented in a chart format (see the sample on p. 7). The charts have been designed so that for each standard a list of states with similarly worded standards is included and some common early childhood classroom practices are identified where that standard may be addressed. Then what the children might show in their progress toward that standard is delineated into three categories of progress. Finally, some curricular suggestions for activities and teacher interactions are given for each progress category.

In addition, at the end of each chapter with the charts, the content standards addressed will be looked at in light of the learning areas in a preschool classroom, as well as in projects that follow upon children's interests, and in large and small group times.

Communicating with others about standards will be the focus of chapter 11, while improving child outcomes and remaining an advocate for young children's needs will be addressed in chapter 12.

Throughout this book, a sampling of standards will be used from a variety of states. Many states have very similar standards with different wording or emphasis. If you wish to learn more about your specific state's preschool early learning standards, you can use the Internet and easily access them. Several national organizations have posted information about early learning standards from all across the United States. Here are some Web sites that have information for you:

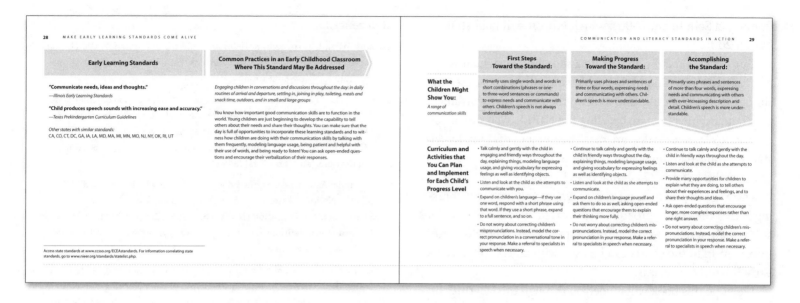

- Early Childhood Education Assessment Consortium, Council of Chief State School Officers, "State Early Learning (Birth to Third Grade) and Early Childhood Program Standards," www.ccsso.org/ECEAstandards

- National Child Care Information Center, www.nccic.org/pubs/goodstart/elgwebsites.html

- National Institute for Early Education Research (NIEER), "State Standards Database," www.nieer.org/standards/statelist.php

The NIEER Web site includes a correlation of state standards by domain or content area. You can click on a specific standard and see a list of states that include that standard. The NIEER Web site is the source that is used to identify similar standards in the charts in this book. Because it was last updated in 2003, there are many states' early learning standards that are not included in this correlation because they were developed after that time. According to Kenneth Robin at NIEER, standards developed since 2003 will be referenced in *The State of Preschool: 2005 State Preschool Yearbook* (Barnett, Hustedt,

Robin and Schulman, 2006), which NIEER will publish in March 2006.

Our belief is that by giving you a sampling of standards from across the nation in this book, you will be able to see the similarities that abound and look up the particular wording of the standard in your state by using the NIEER Web site or your own state's standards documents. The uniqueness of individual states is indeed an important aspect of the educational system in the United States. Good practices for young children are, however, good practices no matter where you live! Our thinking is that the child's progress and curricular recommendations still remain much the same from state to state. Therefore, the information in the charts can be used with any set of preschool early learning standards.

We hope this book will guide you through the labyrinth of information out there about preschool early learning standards and provide you with a clear path that allows you to use them to their fullest benefit and truly help young children reach their full potential!

References

Barnett, W. S., J. T. Hustedt, K. B. Robin, and K. L. Schulman. 2006. *The state of preschool: 2005 state preschool yearbook.* New Brunswick, NJ: National Institute for Early Education Research.

Early Childhood Education Assessment Consortium, Council of Chief State School Officers. 2005. The words we use: A glossary of terms for early childhood education standards and assessment. www.ccsso.org/projects/SCASS/projects/early_childhood_education_assessment_consortium/publications_and_products/2840.cfm.

The National Association for the Education of Young Children (NAEYC) and the National Association of Early Childhood Specialists in State Departments of Education (NAECS/SDE). 2002. Early learning standards: Creating the conditions for success. www.naeyc.org/about/positions/pdf/position_statement.pdf.

Scott-Little, Catherine, Sharon Lynn Kagan, and Victoria Stebbins Frelow. 2004. Inside the content: The breadth and depth of early learning standards. *SERVE's expanded learning opportunities national leadership area.* Greensboro, NC: SERVE. www.serve.org

Shore, Rima, Elena Bodrova, and Deborah Leong. 2004. Child outcome standards in pre-K programs: What are standards; what is needed to make them work? *Preschool Policy Matters* (National Institute for Early Education Research), no. 5.

Planning Curriculum with Early Learning Standards in Mind

As an early educator you already incorporate learning standards in all that you do with children. Whether you are aware of it or not, everything you do with them contributes to their learning about the world and their place in it. As you help children with everyday tasks and routines, you are modeling ways to take care of their needs and helping them develop the skills and independence to do so. When you talk with children, you are helping develop their vocabulary and use of language. When you read and sing to them, you are broadening their awareness of the many ways that human beings express their feelings, impart information, or describe the wonders of life. When you join them in their play at the water table or the block area, you are helping them develop understanding of quantities and learn more about the properties of water and the challenges of construction.

Early educators have long identified goals for the children in their care. Early learning standards are now defining those goals more specifically from state to state. So, for a child in Massachusetts, the goals will be tied to the Pre-K Standards in the Massachusetts Curriculum Frameworks, while for a child in Illinois, the goals will be tied to the Illinois Early Learning Standards, and so on around the country.

What Is Curriculum for Preschoolers?

Teaching young children looks different than teaching older children. And for good reason! Young children are active. They do not listen well. They are learning to get along in a group. They are figuring out how to channel their energies, control their behavior, take care of themselves, and use their language to get what they need. They are dependent on caring adults to establish a safe and supportive atmosphere for them where they can learn more about relating with others and feel comfortable taking risks and trying new things.

As you work with young children, you are shaping what kind of student each child will be in his or her later schooling. In addition, you are giving children information about the world: nature, their bodies, their families, their communities. And you are providing opportunities for children to begin to figure out the process of reading, the concepts of mathematics, and the vocabulary of the sciences. There is a lot going on in early childhood curriculum—far more than can probably be captured in one set of early learning standards!

Many outside of the field of early childhood education advocate for increasing attention to the development of academic skills of young children. But caution is in order. Not all recommendations are based on an understanding of the best practices for teaching young children.

> Increased attention to academic skills is not a problem as long as it does not come at the expense of attention to social skills, emotional well-being, and other resources. . . . Rigidly paced, curriculum-driven, scripted instruction that is not developmentally appropriate . . . will not promote many of the academic skills. . . . Moreover, many studies have shown that this kind of instruction can undermine young children's motivation to learn.

> Effective teaching cannot be delivered through a one-size-fits-all or scripted instructional program. Good teachers know well what each child knows and understands, and they use that knowledge to plan appropriate and varied learning opportunities that are embedded in contexts and activities that make sense to young children. (Stipek 2005, 3)

What is special and unique about an appropriate early childhood approach to curriculum is the way in which learning experiences are planned and implemented. It is in the "how" that early care and education is distinctive from the education in later grades. And, even with the development of early learning standards around the country, educational experts are nearly unanimous in their support of maintaining the uniqueness of curriculum in programs for young children. "Within a rich, play-based curriculum, early childhood educators can implement the expectations of early learning standards, including language, literacy, and other academic content" (Hyson 2004, 6).

In an article titled "Rigorous Academics in Preschool and Kindergarten? Yes! Let Me Tell You How" (Gronlund 2001) I explained the "how" of implementing learning and academics for young children. You can find this article printed in full in the appendix of this book. Many early educators report that they use this article with parents and community members who question the value of play and exploration for children.

The key point in the article is that good early childhood practices incorporate learning, academics, and standards into play with purpose and intent. This play is not random or completely out of the control of the teachers because they have carefully planned many aspects that will direct the play to be more positive, more interesting to the children, and more ripe for learning opportunities. More purposeful and productive play will result when you plan

- the setup of the environment;
- the kinds of materials that are available;
- long periods of time for exploration and a balance between active and quiet activities in the flow of the daily schedule;
- the manner in which the adults will be interacting with the children as guides, as co-players, as instructors, or as observers;
- to follow the children's interests, and yet always be ready to step in and take advantage of teachable moments;
- goals for the children's learning and development, goals for the whole group, and goals for individual children;
- to observe the children to see how they are progressing toward those goals.

Quality preschool programs embrace curriculum that recognizes that young children need lots of activity, manipulation of objects, interaction with caring adults and peers, exposure to books, music, and nature, and opportunities to play indoors and

out. They may use a combination of curricular approaches that incorporate the following:

- Learning areas or centers
- A balance between child-directed play and exploration and teacher-led small and large groups
- Content that is sometimes determined by the teacher and sometimes determined by the children's interests
- Recognition that learning occurs even in daily routines such as arrival and departure, snacks and meals, hand washing, toileting, cleanup, and transitions from activity to activity

Ways to Think about Standards in a Preschool Curriculum

How can early learning standards come alive in a preschool classroom? How can they fit into learning areas, play, teacher-led groups, and daily routines? There are two ways to think about standards in a preschool curriculum: naturalistically and intentionally.

Naturalistic Approaches

Naturalistically, standards are infused in all that goes on. You can look back over the day with the children and think about what you saw children do and heard them say. You can identify what standards were imbedded in playful activities like dramatic play in the house corner or painting at the easel. You can even find standards that were addressed as children washed their hands or put their coats on to go outdoors! As you become more familiar with your state's early learning standards you can begin to see how children are continually working toward those goals. Thinking about standards naturalistically requires conscientious attention to what children are doing and familiarity with your early learning standards. It also requires some form of reflection—whether in discussion with your colleagues or in written observations and recording. Here is an example:

In Lisa and Roseanne's classroom of four-year-olds, two girls, Hannah and Ling, played in the dramatic play area for approximately twenty-five minutes. Lisa observed them as they tried on various hats, dresses, capes, and shoes and looked at themselves often in the mirror. At one point, Ling was wearing a crown of flowers. Hannah tugged the crown off of Ling's head. Ling smiled, fixed her hair, and did not protest. She just got another hat. Then Hannah found a plastic lunchbox. She opened it up and started to put play food items in it. Ling went to the play refrigerator and passed food items to Hannah, announcing what each one was as she did so. "Apple, orange, banana, hot dog." As Hannah put the hot dog in the lunchbox, she said, "No, that's not a fruit," and took it out.

Lisa and Roseanne met after the morning session for a few minutes before heading to lunch. Lisa told Roseanne about the scene she had witnessed with the girls. As they talked, they realized that many early learning standards had been addressed in the play. Together, they made an oral list of standards, which included the following:

- *Using language to converse*
- *Dressing and undressing self*
- *Playing and cooperating with another child*
- *For Ling, getting along with a friend without conflict*
- *For Hannah, sorting and categorizing*

These standards had been imbedded in the girls' play. By observing them, Lisa witnessed their progress toward these standards. She could then write anecdotes or observation notes to put in a portfolio, or make a note on a checklist so that she could keep a record of each girl's achievement related to the standards. This happened naturalistically, as part of the everyday curriculum in this preschool classroom.

Intentional Approaches

Thinking intentionally about standards is a more proactive process. You can plan for activities and materials that will directly address specific early learning standards. Planning intentionally for standards may involve several steps ahead of time. You may

- put together specific materials or activities to address that standard;

- write the goals on a lesson or activity plan;

- plan for how you will record what the children do in relation to that standard.

When being intentional about incorporating early learning standards, you may choose specific materials or plan a certain activity that is tied directly to one or more standards. That activity may be something that occurs in one of your learning areas and still allows the children to be more child-directed as they participate in it. In that case, you may serve as a guide or role model, and then observe what the children do. Here is an example:

···

Robin and Whitney teach three-year-olds. In their early learning standards, they noted that interest in books and book-handling skills such as holding the book correctly, turning one page at a time, and scanning from left to right were included. They already had a library area in their room and had noticed that various children went over there during Activity Time. Robin suggested that they make this area a little more enticing so that they could really focus on children's skills in relation to this standard. Whitney suggested that they take the crown and cape out of the dress-up area and place them in the library on a special chair. Then any child who wished could go to the library area and be the "King or Queen Reader." They agreed that they would need to take turns observing who chose to join in this activity and then make notes about that child's book-handling skills.

When they introduced the idea of King and Queen Readers to the children, they immediately had several enthusiastic volunteers, so many that they had to make a waiting list of the children's names to ensure that everyone would get a chance. As Whitney or Robin observed each child, they took brief notes about the child's handling of the book and awareness of the reading process. Luke held the book appropriately and made up his own story, which was not related to the actual book at all. He occasionally turned the pages, sometimes from front to back and sometimes from back to front. Mario also held the book appropriately and carefully studied each picture, making up a story that was related to what he saw in each picture, turning pages one at a time. Anika chose a book with which she was very familiar. She held the book in front of her as a teacher would do, showing the other children gathered around. Her eyes scanned the pages from left to right, and occasionally, her finger pointed along under the words on the page as she recounted the story accurately, almost word for word. By setting up this activity, Robin and Whitney learned much about how each child was progressing in his or her book handling and early reading skills.

···

There will be times when you set up a teacher-led activity where you directly instruct and model for the children, teaching them the information or modeling for them the skill you are working toward. Again, you observe them as you interact with them so that you can see how they are acquiring that skill or understanding the concepts involved. Here are two examples:

....

Brenta decided that she wanted to introduce the concept of measurement to her children in her mixed-age classroom of three-, four-, and five-year-olds. She had noticed that they already identified which blocks were longer than others and which children were taller or shorter. She also knew that introducing children to comparison and measurement tools was a part of the mathematics early learning standards in her state. She planned a series of activities around measurement for the week that included the following:

- *Introducing children to the concept at large group time*

- *Giving them opportunities to work directly with her on a variety of measurement activities during exploration time*

- *Following up on those activities when the children gathered again at large group times*

Brenta began by introducing the children to a piece of string, a stack of connecting cubes, a ruler, and a meter stick. She showed them how they could hold any of these items next to another item and identify whether the item was longer, shorter, or the same size. She then put these items out at exploration time and helped children as they measured and compared items around the room. Another day, she announced that she was going to cut a piece of string as long as each child's body so that they could measure things in the room that were just the same size as they were. At exploration time, she had a lineup of participants eagerly awaiting their turn to be measured. Then off they went with their strings, measuring everything in sight. At the follow-up group time, Brenta asked them to tell the group what they measured in the room that was the same length as their string and recorded their answers on a large sheet of chart paper. On another day, Brenta suggested that children use the connecting blocks to measure the table, the height of the chairs, or the length of their arms or feet. She helped children count how many blocks were needed for each of these items and recorded their results for them. The week went on, and the interest in measurement was still high, so activities continued over the next two weeks, with children moving to using the rulers and meter sticks as well. Throughout all of these activities, Brenta made brief notes about individual children's understanding of the measurement concepts related to the math early learning standards that she was incorporating.

————

Linnea works in a program that identifies its curriculum as "Reggio-inspired." She and her colleagues attempt to engage the children around topics or projects that often originate from the children's interests. Once a topic is identified, Linnea carefully plans for a series of activities that will help the children explore the topic in depth, learning the concepts and vocabulary associated with that topic. Once again, early learning standards can be easily imbedded in these activities. Whether the topic is balls or gardening or construction machines, almost all of the early learning standards can be addressed in some way throughout these investigative studies.

Incorporating Standards in a Lesson or Activity Plan

On a lesson or activity plan, many early educators tend to state an activity and then list the materials that they will use. To help be more clear and focused and more intentional in incorporating and addressing goals and standards, you can go beyond a materials list.

> It is not necessary to list all of the materials involved, nor is such a listing helpful to the planning process. Instead, by writing down your goals for the learning area, you will keep yourself focused on the purposes for activities and the ways you and your teaching colleagues can support learning and development. Each goal can then be directly correlated with expectations for preschool children's performance and tied to assessment information.
> (Gronlund 2003, 26)

Here's an example of a weekly planning framework with goals identified for the learning areas and various activities. This plan is taken from the book *Focused Early Learning: A Planning Framework for Teaching Young Children* (Gronlund 2003).

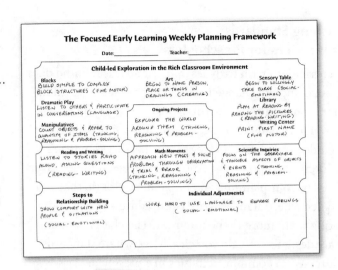

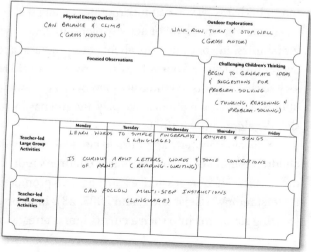

Early Learning Standards and Best Practices for Preschoolers

Planning curriculum with early learning standards in mind does not require a complete change in teaching practices. Providing play, exploration, and active learning opportunities and recognizing the value in daily routines and the importance of caring adults as guides and observers are still the best ways to teach young children. Incorporating standards requires adding a layer of awareness to your planning and implementation so that you can clearly see where standards are being addressed and add ways to bring them more to the forefront. The charts in later chapters are designed to help you clearly see where standards can be addressed in common activities in a preschool classroom. In that way, you can incorporate the language of those standards in your lesson or activity plans, in your newsletters for families, in your publicity about your program, and in your own thinking about your role as an early educator. This is necessary so that parents, community members, and policymakers understand that what looks like play and fun has learning and skill development within it.

"A developmentally appropriate curriculum for young children is child centered, embraces children's individual differences, encourages active learning, and promotes deep understanding" (Geist and Baum 2005, 28). Incorporating early learning standards into such a curriculum is already occurring.

Becoming aware and intentional about it and communicating clearly through plans, conversations, newsletters, and presentations are important steps to take so that others see the ways in which the children's learning is central to all that occurs in early childhood programs. The charts in chapters 4 through 10 should help with that process. And in chapter 11, more ideas about communicating with others about early learning standards will be addressed.

References

Geist, Eugene, and Angela C. Baum. 2005. *Yeah, but's* that keep teachers from embracing an active curriculum: Overcoming the resistance. *Young Children* (NAEYC) 60, no. 4.

Gronlund, Gaye. 2003. *Focused early learning: A planning framework for teaching young children*. St. Paul: Redleaf.

Gronlund, Gaye. 2001. Rigorous academics in preschool and kindergarten? Yes! Let me tell you how. *Young Children* (NAEYC) 56, no. 2.

Hyson, Marilou. 2004. From words to sentences: Play as the powerful connection. *Play, Policy, & Practice Connections* (NAEYC) 8, no. 2.

Stipek, Deborah. 2005. Early childhood education at a crossroads: Access to preschool has come a long way, but critical choices lie ahead. *Harvard Education Letter* (July/August): www.edletter.org/past/issues/2005-ja/crossroads.shtml.

Using Authentic Assessment Measures

3

How do you assess children's learning and accomplishments related to standards? The resounding answer from the field of early childhood education is: authentically, authentically, authentically! But just what does authentic assessment mean? How do you do it in such a way that you can

track children's progress toward early learning standards so that you can better teach them? And how do you represent that information for families, for administrators, and policy makers so that you can be accountable to the expectations identified for young children in your state? This chapter will answer those questions.

The Early Childhood Education Assessment Consortium of the Council of Chief State School Officers defines assessment as "a systematic procedure for obtaining information from observation, interviews, portfolios, projects, tests, and other sources that can be used to make judgments about characteristics of children or programs" (www.ccsso.org 2005). They distinguish

authentic assessment as one that does *not* incorporate the use of standardized tests. And they note that as children get older, the reliability and validity of assessment information increases, but that it is not very high for young children.

What does authentic assessment look like in practice, then? Authentic assessment is imbedded in the work you do every day with children. As you interact with them, you are engaged in a constant process of assessment as you

- guide their play and exploration;
- converse with them;
- help them with things that are difficult for them;

- encourage them to try new things;

- join in their excitement when they accomplish something.

You are in a continual process of observing and listening, as well as evaluating what you are seeing and hearing. In the position statement titled "Where We Stand on Curriculum, Assessment, and Program Evaluation," the National Association for the Education of Young Children (NAEYC) and the National Association of Early Childhood Specialists in State Departments of Education (NAECS/SDE) state clear criteria to guide you as an early educator as you assess young children's strengths, progress, and needs. They suggest the use of assessment methods that are

- developmentally appropriate;

- culturally and linguistically responsive;

- tied to children's daily activities;

- inclusive of families;

- done with clear, beneficial purposes in order to inform teaching and learning, to identify concerns that may require intervention, and to improve educational interventions. (NAEYC 2003)

Testing of preschool children is not recommended by any of the organizations referred to earlier. In fact, the CCSSO states,

"Children younger than primary age have not attained the developmental capacity to understand the purposes of formal testing" (www.ccsso.org 2005). Instead, it is recommended that early educators use a combination of methods including observation, work sampling, and parent interviews in order to determine what a child can and cannot do.

These methods involve gathering and evaluating information. You gather information about a child as you work and play with him. You take in a lot of information every day about every child as you watch him, listen to him, ask him open-ended questions to learn more about his thinking, and challenge him to try the next step.

Your next step, then, is to evaluate all of the information you have learned about the child. This is where early learning standards come into play. They are the reference by which the child's accomplishments are measured. You ask yourself the following questions:

- Has the child accomplished each particular standard or not?

- If not, where is he on a spectrum of progress toward accomplishing that standard?

- If he has accomplished the standard, what is the next step in acquisition of skills and knowledge that he is ready for?

- What curricular plans will best meet this child where he is and help him to move on in his progress and accomplishments?

This assessment process of observing children and relating those observations to standards is most in line with the definitions and recommendations noted by the national organizations mentioned earlier.

Documentation

There are many ways for you to consider documenting the information you are gathering through your observations so that you can remember and refer to it later when you are ready to evaluate it related to standards. You may do one of the following:

- Watch and take in the information visually, mentally reviewing how it fits in with other things you have learned about this child.
- Take quick, brief notes to jog your memory later.
- Work out a system with your colleagues where one member of the team can sit to the side of activities for a brief period of time and take formal anecdotal notes. These are usually more extensive in nature and may include quotes of the children's use of language and more detailed descriptions of their actions. (For many documentation ideas, see *Focused Observations: How to Observe Children for Assessment and Curriculum Planning*, Gronlund and James, 2005.)

- Take a photograph of the child engaged in constructing with blocks or reading a book.
- Use a tape recorder or video camera to capture more fully what the child is saying or doing.
- Ask the child if you can keep a work sample such as a painting, a drawing, or a writing sample so that you have additional documentation to support the evaluation you will do related to early learning standards.

These mental and written observations, audio and videotapes, and work samples are organized in a systematic way so that each child has a folder, notebook, or portfolio of documentation that represents what she is learning and how she is growing in her skills and knowledge.

Evaluation

Once the collection and documentation of information is under way, the evaluation process can begin. This process involves reviewing the documentation and deciding what standards are addressed in the child's performance. In some states, tools have been provided to help streamline the documentation and evaluation processes. For example, in Illinois, PDAs (personal digital assistants), or handheld devices, have been given to early educators with the Illinois Early Learning Standards programmed into them. As an educator observes children in action, she can check off standards in the child's file on the PDA. In California, forms are available to download from a state Web site (www.cde.ca.gov/sp/cd/ci/drdpforms.asp). The Developmental Profiles can be used to track children's accomplishments of specific items on the state's Desired Results. In New Mexico, child care programs that are funded by the Office of Child Development are required to use a format that combines the documentation of gathered information with the evaluation process. This method is called "Focused Portfolios" and involves a format that includes observation notes of children in action and identification of early learning standards (Gronlund and Engel 2001). Here is an example of a completed Focused Portfolios Developmental Milestones Collection Form. Notice that the standard is identified on the same form as the observation information. Sometimes a photo or a work sample might be included to round out the documentation. You can check with your state to find out what tools or documentation methodology is recommended for you.

One of the frustrations of working with young children is that you may not always see the clear accomplishment of a standard. As we discussed in chapter 1, early childhood is the time to work on foundational skills, to help children acquire the capabilities to be effective learners and students in the later years. You will not necessarily see preschoolers learning to read, for example. But you will be working with them on learning to love and value books for the information and stimulation they provide. You will

---

Developmental Milestones Collection Form
Version #1 Preschooler

Child's Name _Nicholas_   Age _4_
Observer _Maria_   Date _4/16/99_

Check off the *areas of development*
that apply:

☐ Thinking, Reasoning & Problem-Solving
☑ Emotional and Social Competency
☐ Gross-Motor Development
☐ Fine-Motor Development
☐ Language and Communication
☐ Reading & Writing Development
☐ Creative Development

This photo, work sample and/or anecdote illustrates the following *developmental milestone(s)*:

Can sense a person's feelings and has some ideas how to help.

Check off whatever applies to the context of this observation:

☑ Child-initiated activity   ☐ Done with adult guidance
☐ Teacher-initiated activity   ☑ Done with peer(s)
☐ New task for this child   ☑ Time spent (1-5 mins.)
☑ Familiar task for this child   ☐ Time spent (5-15 mins.)
☐ Done independently   ☐ Time spent (15+ mins.)

Anecdotal Note: Describe what you saw the child do and/or heard the child say.

Jessica and Darianne were fighting over the dolls. Nicholas saw them fighting. He picked up the extra doll and tried to hand it to Darianne. I heard him say "Darianne you can have this one."

be teaching them how to handle books, how to look at the illustrations, to listen carefully as someone reads, to ask questions and make predictions, and to enjoy the rhythm of the language. You will be helping them to learn that print has meaning and can be decoded—even though you may not see them do this actual decoding. When assessing children's capabilities in relation to early learning standards, you are evaluating their progress toward the ultimate goal of reading (or mathematical computation, or scientific experimentation, and so on).

So, once you have identified the standards that the child is working on, your next task is to decide how the child is progressing in accomplishing that standard. This decision may happen immediately as you witness the child's actions. Or it may need to be determined through reflection over time after you have been able to observe the child's performance on more than one occasion. In the charts in this book you will see that a child's progress toward accomplishing a standard is measured by three steps:

1. First steps toward the standard

2. Making progress toward the standard

3. Accomplishing the standard

These three steps correlate with the way some states are asking for information to be reported. In Minnesota and Illinois, for example, the recommended authentic assessment system is The Work Sampling System.® Within the Developmental Guidelines for this assessment are three rating possibilities for each of the performance indicators. Those ratings are Not Yet, In Process, and Proficient (Dichtelmiller et. al. 2001). On the California Desired Results Developmental Profiles, four ratings are included: Not Yet, Emerging, Almost Mastered, Fully Mastered.

Not all children will accomplish every early learning standard. Instead, they will show variability in their capabilities with strengths in some areas and weaknesses in others. If only two ratings were included, such as Accomplished and Not Accomplished, small steps toward an early learning standard would be completely lost and many children would appear to be failing. In using three or four ratings, early educators can identify more clearly just where the child stands in relation to the expectation. This will help with planning curriculum for that child and give a more accurate picture of the child's progress than a simple "Yes" or "No" related to a standard.

Looking at Children's Performance Related to Standards

Here are some examples of how children show their progress related to standards about writing and problem solving. You will have the opportunity to read through teacher observation notes, look at some work samples and photos, and evaluate the evidence related to a preschool standard about writing and one about mathematical problem solving. Three examples will be given for each standard showing the child's first steps toward the standard, the child's progress toward the standard, and the child's accomplishment of the standard.

....

1. In the Arkansas Early Childhood Education Framework, Devel-opmental Learning Strand 3 *includes benchmarks related to Cognitive/Intellectual Learning. Specifically under Language Arts, Benchmark 3.6 states, "Demonstrates an interest in using writing for a purpose."*

....

A Child Making First Steps toward the Standard

Luis (3 years 7 months) was at the writing table and chose several different colored markers and wrote with his left hand in a correct pencil grasp. When Luis was done, he said, "Look, teacher. I wrote my name—Luis!"

Luis scribbled all over his paper and identified specific marks as writing his name. He is showing that he understands that there are ways to represent his name in writing even though he doesn't have the capability to do so by writing letters in a recognizable way yet.

A Child Showing Progress toward the Standard

Forest went to the table where there was lined paper, construction paper, markers, and pencils and announced, "I'm going to make a book." For five to ten minutes, he wrote and drew with his right hand. A teacher asked Forest if he wanted her to write some words for him. Forest agreed. "This says, 'This is for my sister,'" he dictated as he traced his finger underneath his writing. The teacher wrote the words for him.

Forest shows that he understands that books contain writing. His writing includes letterlike shapes and some letters from his name, as well as scribble writing that looks like cursive writing. He confirmed his understanding that the writing had meaning when he dictated that meaning for the teacher to write.

A Child Accomplishing the Standard

Wyatte (5 years 0 months) drew a picture of herself to put into a class book, "The Important Book." She said, "I wrote letters in an open book." She also signed her name. A little later in the day, she was talking about the sun and how it was her favorite planet. Using a firm pincer grasp, she wrote "son" by sounding out the letters all by herself.

Wyatte shows that she knows writing is in books and is made up of letters. She even had the fine motor control to make them very small and fit them in her drawing! She wrote her name correctly and in a recognizable fashion. And she figured out the letters to write a word she did not know ("sun") by sounding them out and making the sound-letter connection. In all of these examples, she shows her understanding of writing for a purpose and her capabilities to do so.

2. In the mathematical area of the Nevada Pre-Kindergarten Standards, *problem solving is addressed in Process Standard 6.0 as follows:*

> *Students will develop their ability to solve problems by engaging in developmentally appropriate problem-solving opportunities in which there is a need to use various approaches to investigate and understand mathematical concepts in order to: formulate their own problems; find solutions to problems from everyday situations; develop and apply strategies to solve a wide variety of problems; and integrate mathematical reasoning, communication and connections.*

Then, under that Process Standard, the following benchmark is identified:

> *Benchmark 6.6 E/L*
> *Try more than one strategy when the first strategy proves to be unproductive.*

A Child Making First Steps toward the Standard

A few puzzles are on the floor. "It's a rainbow fish," Jenna (3 years 11 months) declares as she dumps out the ten-piece puzzle. The first time Jenna tries the puzzle, she attempts to put one piece at a time, trying every spot until it fits. The second time she does the same puzzle, she quickly places the first two pieces, and then tries every other piece in every spot on the puzzle until it fits. She then tries an eight-piece puzzle, and again uses the same strategy of trying each piece until it fits. Jenna finishes the puzzle and goes outside.

Jenna has one strategy, using trial and error over and over again, but has not moved on to trying any other ways to figure out how to fit the pieces.

A Child Showing Progress toward the Standard

Today, Erin (4 years 5 months) chose to make designs using the geoboard and rubber bands. She announced, "I want to make a house," but ran out of room on two attempts to do so with rubber bands on a single geoboard. Her teacher suggested that she try to make a smaller house. Erin thought for a minute. "Oh, I know," she said, and positioned a second board next to the first one. "I think I can make a really big house now, but I don't want to break a rubber band because it hurts." She then took larger rubber bands off of another board and said, "These might not break and I can make a really big house." She used both boards and made several other designs.

Erin is showing flexibility in her thinking and trying two different strategies as she solves the problem of making a house on her geoboard and looks ahead at possible results (rubber bands breaking). She then finds the best materials (larger rubber bands) and carries out her plan. This logical thinking will help her solve many mathematical problems in the future.

A Child Accomplishing the Standard

Karlee (3 years 10 months) was at the table playing with eighty or so plastic colored bear counters. Her teacher asked her, "Karlee, what are you going to do with so many bears?" She said, "I'm going to put them together, and then actually going to count them and then play with them after I count them." She sorted all of the bears by color correctly. Then she said, "There's too many. I can't count all of these." Her teacher asked, "What do you need to do so you can count them?" She sat for a minute and then said, "I'll stand them up so I can count them." She stood them up and counted each group of colored bears, saying the numbers out loud. She maintained her one-to-one correspondence by touching each bear as she counted. She was accurate up to seven bears with the red and blue ones, six with the yellow ones, and eight with the green ones. After those numbers, she skipped some numbers in her counting sequence and did not touch each bear as she said a number.

Karlee uses many strategies to solve problems in her play with the counting bears: She sorts by color, she puzzles about how to count them, she stands them up to help herself with the counting process, and she touches each bear as she counts up to the quantities at which she can maintain one-to-one correspondence. She has accomplished this standard in the number of ways she went about solving the problems that evolved in her play with these materials.

The Assessment and Curriculum Planning Process

Assessment and curriculum planning go hand in hand. As you observe and learn more about children's progress toward standards, you are continually making decisions about what to do next for each one. The following chart shows the integration of assessment and curriculum planning (Gronlund and James 2005, 96).

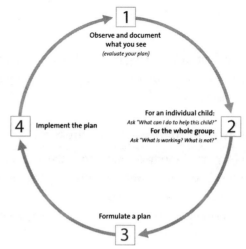

References

Dichtelmiller, Margo L., Judy R. Jablon, Dorthea B. Marsden, Samuel J. Meisels. 2001. The work sampling system developmental guidelines. 4th Edition. Parsippany, NJ: Pearson Early Learning.

Early Childhood Education Assessment Consortium, Council of Chief State School Officers. 2005. The words we use: A glossary of terms for early childhood education standards and assessment. www.ccsso.org/projects/SCASS/projects/early_childhood_education_assessment_consortium/publications_and_products/2840.cfm.

Gronlund, Gaye, and Bev Engel. 2001. Focused portfolios: A complete assessment for the young child. St. Paul: Redleaf.

Gronlund, Gaye, and Marlyn James. 2005. *Focused observations: How to observe children for assessment and curriculum planning.* St. Paul: Redleaf.

The National Association for the Education of Young Children (NAEYC) and the National Association of Early Childhood Specialists in State Departments of Education (NAECS/SDE). 2003. Where we stand on curriculum, assessment, and program evaluation. www.naeyc.org/about/positions/cape.asp.

Communication and Literacy Standards in Action

4

Communication among humans primarily takes place through speaking and listening and through the written word. Early learning standards in the area of language arts include children's expressive and receptive language—how do they speak to others and how are their listening skills developing? In addition, the standards address their growing interest in listening to books and reading them on their own, recognizing that the actual process of decoding and reading will come at a later age than preschool. However, beginning to recognize alphabet letters and names of themselves and their friends will be evident and can be expected. In addition, growing awareness of the sounds of language is an important foundation for later acquisition of reading skills. Finally, learning to write in order to communicate with others is another part of the language arts standards.

In this chapter, we have chosen eight standards from different states that cover the range of communication and literacy early learning standards around the country. We recognize that there are many more ways to address these standards than the ideas we have put forth here. We invite you to think about your classroom and curriculum. How will you address these standards in your program?

Early Learning Standards	**Common Practices in an Early Childhood Classroom Where This Standard May Be Addressed**

"Communicate needs, ideas and thoughts."

—*Illinois Early Learning Standards*

"Child produces speech sounds with increasing ease and accuracy."

—*Texas Prekindergarten Curriculum Guidelines*

Other states with similar standards:
CA, CO, CT, DC, GA, IA, LA, MD, MA, MI, MN, MO, NJ, NY, OK, RI, UT

Engaging children in conversations and discussions throughout the day: in daily routines of arrival and departure, settling in, joining in play, toileting, meals and snack time, outdoors, and in small and large groups

You know how important good communication skills are to function in the world. Young children are just beginning to develop the capability to tell others about their needs and share their thoughts. You can make sure that the day is full of opportunities to incorporate these learning standards and to witness how children are doing with their communication skills by talking with them frequently, modeling language usage, being patient and helpful with their use of words, and being ready to listen! You can ask open-ended questions and encourage their verbalization of their responses.

Access state standards at www.ccsso.org/ECEAstandards. For information correlating state standards, go to www.nieer.org/standards/statelist.php.

	First Steps Toward the Standard:	**Making Progress Toward the Standard:**	**Accomplishing the Standard:**
What the Children Might Show You: *A range of communication skills*	Primarily uses single words and words in short combinations (phrases or one- to three-word sentences or commands) to express needs and communicate with others. Children's speech is not always understandable.	Primarily uses phrases and sentences of three or four words, expressing needs and communicating with others. Children's speech is more understandable.	Primarily uses phrases and sentences of more than four words, expressing needs and communicating with others with ever-increasing description and detail. Children's speech is more understandable.
Curriculum and Activities that You Can Plan and Implement for Each Child's Progress Level	• Talk calmly and gently with the child in engaging and friendly ways throughout the day, explaining things, modeling language usage, and giving vocabulary for expressing feelings as well as identifying objects. • Listen and look at the child as she attempts to communicate with you. • Expand on children's language—if they use one word, respond with a short phrase using that word. If they use a short phrase, expand to a full sentence, and so on. • Do not worry about correcting children's mispronunciations. Instead, model the correct pronunciation in a conversational tone in your response. Make a referral to specialists in speech when necessary.	• Continue to talk calmly and gently with the child in friendly ways throughout the day, explaining things, modeling language usage, and giving vocabulary for expressing feelings as well as identifying objects. • Listen and look at the child as she attempts to communicate. • Expand on children's language yourself and ask them to do so as well, asking open-ended questions that encourage them to explain their thinking more fully. • Do not worry about correcting children's mispronunciations. Instead, model the correct pronunciation in your response. Make a referral to specialists in speech when necessary.	• Continue to talk calmly and gently with the child in friendly ways throughout the day. • Listen and look at the child as she attempts to communicate. • Provide many opportunities for children to explain what they are doing, to tell others about their experiences and feelings, and to share their thoughts and ideas. • Ask open-ended questions that encourage longer, more complex responses rather than one right answer. • Do not worry about correcting children's mispronunciations. Instead, model the correct pronunciation in your response. Make a referral to specialists in speech when necessary.

Early Learning Standards

Common Practices in an Early Childhood Classroom Where This Standard May Be Addressed

"Children show progress in listening when they follow directions that involve a two or three-step sequence of actions."

—*Minnesota Early Childhood Indicators of Progress*

Other states with similar standards:
CA, CO, DC, GA, IL, IA, LA, MA, MI, MN, MO, NY, OK, RI, TX, UT

Giving children clear and simple directions in the course of everyday activities and routines, starting with one step and moving on to two or more steps as their understanding increases

Young children are not good listeners. They are easily distracted because they are so interested in the world around them. Listening closely enough to follow two- and three-step sequenced directions takes focus and opportunities for practice. As adults, we need to be patient and consistent in our recognition of this developing skill.

Begin with one-step directions such as "Please sit here" or "Get your backpack." As you see consistent follow-through, you can add another step. For example, "Please wash your hands and sit down for snack." If you see a child having difficulty following through, break the task down into one step until you see consistent success. Always build on success rather than continue with failure!

	First Steps Toward the Standard:	Making Progress Toward the Standard:	Accomplishing the Standard:
What the Children Might Show You: *Response to one direction increasing to the capability to follow through with multiple steps*	Follows through with one clear, simple direction	Follows through with two clear, simple directions	Follows through with more than two directions that become increasingly complex and may be accomplished over longer periods of time
Curriculum and Activities that You Can Plan and Implement for Each Child's Progress Level	• Make sure that you have the child's attention by using his name, making eye contact, and stating the direction clearly. • Give the child time to follow through, or repeat the request a second time. If still no response, walk the child through the action: "Now, we'll put your hands in the water to get them all clean." • Encourage the child's follow-through by describing what she's doing, "Look, you're drinking your milk just like I asked you to!"	• As a child consistently follows one direction, start adding a second simple, logical step. "Come to the sink and wash your hands." • If the child is unsuccessful, break the task down into one step at a time. • Give the child time to follow through, or repeat the request a second time. If still no response, walk the child through the action: "Now, we'll walk you over to the sink and put your hands in the water to get them all clean." • Encourage the child's follow-through by describing what she's doing in both steps.	• Start adding a third simple, logical step. "Come to the sink, wash your hands, and go sit down for snack." • If the child is unsuccessful, break the task down into one or two steps at a time. • Give the child time to follow through, or repeat the request a second time. • Encourage the child's follow-through by describing what she's doing in all of the steps. • Increase your expectations for the child's capability of following multiple directions over longer periods of time. Always be ready to back up if necessary!

Early Learning Standards	Common Practices in an Early Childhood Classroom Where This Standard May Be Addressed

"Listen to a wide variety of age appropriate literature read aloud."

—*Massachusetts Early Childhood Indicators of Progress*

Other states with similar standards:
CA, CO, CT, IL, IA, LA, MD, MI, MN, MO, NY, RI, TX, UT

Reading stories with individuals and groups of children

You read stories and books throughout each day—one-on-one with a child on your lap or to a small group of children. Or you read a big book to a large group. You choose books that engage children with interesting story lines and illustrations or photos. You vary the selection with books with no print or little print and those with more print on the page. You make sure to include rhyming books; predictable pattern books; familiar fairy tales and nursery rhymes; nonfiction books about nature, people, and places; funny books; sad books; etc.

Access state standards at www.ccsso.org/ECEAstandards. For information correlating state standards, go to www.nieer.org/standards/statelist.php.

	First Steps Toward the Standard:	**Making Progress Toward the Standard:**	**Accomplishing the Standard:**
What the Children Might Show You: *A range of listening skills and attention to the features of the book*	Listens for a few minutes or does not interact with the book in any way	Listens for longer time periods (five minutes or more) or responds by pointing at pictures, turning pages, or asking simple questions	Listens longer and responds by asking related questions or making pertinent comments or predictions; retells stories read
Curriculum and Activities that You Can Plan and Implement for Each Child's Progress Level	• Try more engaging books or let the child choose his favorite. • Read with the child individually in a quiet, protected area so there are fewer distractions. • Choose pop-up books or books that require physical interaction (pushing a button, pulling a string). • Do not force the child to stay beyond his attention span so that a power struggle develops and the reading experience becomes a negative one.	• Let the child choose favorites and reread familiar books. Continue to increase length of the books. • Give the child responsibility for turning pages or holding the book. • Ask open-ended questions as you read, such as "What do you think will happen?" "Where is he going?" • Model making related comments: "I wonder if his mommy knows he's looking for her." "That caterpillar ate a lot of different types of food!" • Comment on the child's listening and interaction with the story; give encouragement. • Point out where the words are in the book and interesting features in the illustrations.	• Expand the repertoire of books read—include fiction, nonfiction, short, long, predictable, plot-driven, fantasy, serious, funny, informational, etc. • Continue to increase the length of the books. • Still let the child choose favorites and reread familiar books. Encourage the child to tell what will happen next, to follow along with print, or to retell the story in his own words. • Talk about plot and characters. • Point out conventions of print, specific letters and words, stylistic aspects (rhymes, punctuation, etc.). • Comment on the child's listening and comprehension; give encouragement and assurance that he will learn to read as he grows.

Early Learning Standards	Common Practices in an Early Childhood Classroom Where This Standard May Be Addressed

"Demonstrates knowledge of the alphabet."

—*Kentucky Early Childhood Standards*

Other states with similar standards:
CA, DC, IL, MD, MA, MO, NY, OK, RI, TX, UT

Surrounding the children with print so that you are presenting the whole alphabet in the early childhood classroom in as many ways as possible

Alphabet letters in isolation do not have meaning to young children. But when they are shown that letters grouped together represent their names, items, and products in their world and tell stories that they love to hear, the alphabet takes on new meaning. Now building children's familiarity with the alphabet has a purpose: to make sense of print around you so that you can figure it out for yourself. It's like cracking a code! Helping children to develop their alphabet knowledge is an important step in the reading process.

Access state standards at www.ccsso.org/ECEAstandards. For information correlating state standards, go to www.nieer.org/standards/statelist.php.

	First Steps Toward the Standard:	**Making Progress Toward the Standard:**	**Accomplishing the Standard:**
What the Children Might Show You: *A growing awareness of the importance of alphabet letters in the reading and writing process*	Shows awareness of ABCs by singing the "ABC" song or pointing to letters on a page, a puzzle, or a toy when asked (but not necessarily with accuracy)	Recognizes at least the first letter of her name and knows that alphabet letters make up words in the environment	Recognizes and names at least some of the letters in his name and other letters in environmental print, books, puzzles, and toys
Curriculum and Activities that You Can Plan and Implement for Each Child's Progress Level	• Sing the alphabet song and all its variations! • Talk about and point to letters in books, on puzzles or toys, on the child's clothing, or in the classroom environment.	• Have alphabet posters, books, puzzles, stampers, and stickers throughout the room so children can be exposed to alphabet letters in many different contexts. • Make name cards and name charts to take attendance and identify helpers for the day. Children love to see their own name in print! • Use your alphabet rug to hop the alphabet, tippy-toe the alphabet, and walk backward on the alphabet.	• It's not necessary to focus on one letter a week or a day. Instead, focus on the whole alphabet as it presents itself in the children's names, in class announcements, in favorite stories, and on environmental signs and labels. • Have an alphabet center with books, puzzles, stampers, and stickers so children can play with alphabet letters in different ways. • Play games with name cards and name charts comparing similarities and differences and number of letters. • Play alphabet games like I Spy and Alphabet Bingo.

Early Learning Standards	Common Practices in an Early Childhood Classroom Where This Standard May Be Addressed

"I. Phonological and Phonemic Awareness

A. Listen to and identify spoken language sounds in the environment

B. Identify and produce spoken words that rhyme (e.g., rhymes, poems, songs, word games) including word families (e.g., c-at, b-at, s-at)

C. Count or tap the number of syllables in multisyllabic words to show awareness of the syllable as a discrete unit

D. Count or tap the number of words in spoken sentences to show awareness of the word as a discrete unit"

—*New York Early Literacy Guidelines: Pre-Kindergarten through Grade 3*

Other states with similar standards:
CO, DC, IL, LA, MA, MN, MO, OK, RI, TX, UT

Singing songs, chanting finger plays, and playing with language in silly ways to help develop children's awareness of rhyming words, syllables, and the sounds of letters

Young children love to be silly! Using silly language will help develop their reading skills as they mature. Make it fun! Laugh and giggle together!

Enjoy it yourself!

Access state standards at www.ccsso.org/ECEAstandards. For information correlating state standards, go to www.nieer.org/standards/statelist.php.

	First Steps Toward the Standard:	**Making Progress Toward the Standard:**	**Accomplishing the Standard:**
What the Children Might Show You: *A growing awareness of the sounds of language*	Responds with pleasure to songs, chants, finger plays, and word play, imitating adults as language skills develop	Responds and joins in with simple songs, chants, finger plays, and word play involving rhyming and sound substitutions	Joins in with songs and chants and initiates word play involving rhyming and sound substitutions. Is beginning to recognize similarities and differences in sounds of words and letters, number of syllables, and the rhythm of language.
Curriculum and Activities that You Can Plan and Implement for Each Child's Progress Level	• Sing and chant with children often. They love rhythm, melody (even off-key!), and the magic of music. • Make a variety of sounds with them, playing a game back and forth encouraging their participation. • Use a child's name and do silly rhymes and songs, changing the initial consonant. • Laugh and enjoy a child's imitation or attempts to repeat a favorite song or chant. • Use finger plays and poems as ways to introduce rhymes and the rhythm of language.	• Make songs, finger plays, and rhythmic chants part of large group times as well as ways to move children through daily routines. Repeat the same ones again and again—letting the children choose their favorites. • Use a child's name and do silly rhymes and songs, changing the initial consonant, such as in Raffi's "Willoby, Wallaby, Woo." • Read poetry and rhyming books to the children on a regular basis.	• Continue to make songs, finger plays, and rhythmic chants part of large group times as well as ways to move children through daily routines. Add ones that require children to fill in the missing rhyme (like Raffi's "Down by the Bay") or figure out the number of syllables. • Do word play with children's names with songs, sound substitutions, comparisons of initial consonants, and rhyming. • Read poetry and rhyming books to the children on a regular basis pointing out characteristics of the sounds of words and letters.

Early Learning Standards	Common Practices in an Early Childhood Classroom Where This Standard May Be Addressed
"Decoding and word recognition begin when a child understands that there is a relationship between letters and sounds, and that letters put together form words." —*Foundations for Young Children to the Indiana Academic Standards* *Other states with similar standards:* CA, CO, DC, IL, LA, MD, MA, MN, MO, NY, OK, RI, TX, UT	*Pointing out the relationship between letters and sounds as you read books with the children, introduce the alphabet or their names, and model writing for various purposes* This is an important part of learning to read, but be careful not to present it to children before they are ready. Instead, respond to their interest and awareness of written language. Once children are recognizing the importance of the alphabet, the next step for them is to decode groups of alphabet letters together and begin to recognize familiar words.

Access state standards at www.ccsso.org/ECEAstandards. For information correlating state standards, go to www.nieer.org/standards/statelist.php.

	First Steps Toward the Standard:	**Making Progress Toward the Standard:**	**Accomplishing the Standard:**
What the Children Might Show You: *A deepening recognition of the sounds that correlate with alphabet letters in order to produce words in spoken and written language*	Shows beginning awareness of similarities and differences in configurations of letters in familiar names and words	Asks questions and/or makes comments about letters and sounds in familiar names and words	Begins to make sense of some unfamiliar words, whether in familiar or predictable books, or by applying some decoding skills
Curriculum and Activities that You Can Plan and Implement for Each Child's Progress Level	• Help children recognize not only their own names, but those of their friends. • Point out repetitious words in books.	• Provide word dictionaries and picture word books of interest to the children. • Talk about letters and their sounds as you read, as you write children's names, as you see an Exit sign or a food label. • Take your cues from their questions and comments. When Jason says, "Hey, that's says 'J' just like in my name!" You know that he's ready to find other words beginning with the letter J.	• Provide simple-to-read books with predictable word choices. • Provide children with opportunities to see words that are important to them written and displayed. "I love you" has always had great importance for young children. Help them learn how to recognize and read key words and phrases. • Begin to teach children the corresponding sounds for alphabet letters with which they are familiar and help them think in terms of decoding through sounding out words phonetically.

Early Learning Standards	Common Practices in an Early Childhood Classroom Where This Standard May Be Addressed

"Uses pretend writing during play activities (e.g., scribbles lines and shapes)"

—California Desired Results for 3 Years through Prekindergarten

Other states with similar standards:
CO, CT, DC, GA, IL, IA, LA, MD, MA, MI, MN, MO, NY, OK, RI, TX, UT

Providing many opportunities for children to play with writing tools and materials throughout the day

Young children love to imitate the adults in their lives. And adults write for many purposes in everyday life. Pretend writing is a way for children to experiment with the writing process before they feel confident in making recognizable letters and words. Even as they scribble, they are developing fine motor skills and their own awareness of the many purposes and reasons for writing in daily life.

	First Steps Toward the Standard:	**Making Progress Toward the Standard:**	**Accomplishing the Standard:**
What the Children Might Show You: Many different ways of imitating adult writing with increasing fine motor control and closer approximations to letter-like shapes or cursive writing	Makes random marks or scribbles for a variety of purposes	Identifies marks or scribbles as writing; shows more control of the writing tool	Purposefully makes marks and scribbles for writing purposes with increasing control of the writing tool evident in the formation of letter-like shapes, perhaps even some letters, and forms of pretend cursive writing
Curriculum and Activities that You Can Plan and Implement for Each Child's Progress Level	• Model for the children how many ways you use writing every day. • Provide a variety of writing tools (markers, crayons, chalk, pens, pencils) and papers for children to experiment with writing. • Be sure to accept their scribbles and shapes as the writing that's just right for their age.	• Add writing tools and materials in the dramatic play area to give children opportunities to imitate writing grocery lists, recipes, letters, and phone messages as well as paying bills. • Be sure to accept their scribbles and shapes as the writing that's just right for their age.	• Set up a Writing Center in the classroom with many types of writing tools and papers. Add name cards, word lists, picture dictionaries, and alphabet posters for copying. • As children begin to be capable of writing recognizable letters, encourage them to do so. But also accept their scribbles and shapes.

Literacy Standards in Preschool Learning Areas

Blocks

Children can

- communicate needs, thoughts, and ideas;
- follow multi-step directions;
- use pretend writing.

As children work together building and constructing, they talk and describe what they are doing, argue and negotiate with each other, and follow through on plans and suggestions. If writing materials are provided, they may label their structures with their names or pretend writing.

Dramatic Play

Children can

- communicate needs, thoughts, and ideas;
- use pretend writing.

Acting out family life and other life experiences requires children to use language extensively. Adding writing materials enriches the play so that imitation of adult writing of grocery lists, telephone messages, etc., can be included.

Manipulatives

Children can

- demonstrate knowledge of alphabet;
- begin to decode sounds.

Many alphabet puzzles and matching games also include pictures of items that begin with specific letters, helping children develop the sound/letter connection.

Class Library

Children can

- listen to a wide variety of literature;
- hear and discriminate the sounds of language;
- begin to decode sounds.

Reading to individual children or to small and large groups of children provides opportunities to engage them in the joy of listening to great literature and the sounds of language.

Literacy Standards Imbedded in Projects That Follow Upon Children's Interests

When first discussing the topic with the children, ask them to tell you what they already know about the topic as well as what they would like to know (communication). As they talk, make lists to model the writing process, sounding out words as you write (sounds of language, decoding). Provide books and other written materials about the topic (listens to literature). Then, as the topic progresses, encourage their documentation of things they are learning through drawings, pretend writing, plays, and presentations.

Literacy Standards That Can Be Imbedded in Large Group Times

Children can

- communicate needs, thoughts, and ideas (e.g., in group discussions);
- follow multi-step directions (e.g., in games like "Simon Says");
- demonstrate knowledge of alphabet (e.g., with alphabet songs and chants);
- listen to a wide variety of literature (i.e., read, read, read!);
- hear and discriminate the sounds of language (e.g., with songs, chants, and poems);
- begin to decode sounds (e.g., as you read, sing, or chant).

Literacy Standards That Can Be Imbedded in Small Group Work:

Children can

- communicate needs, thoughts, and ideas (e.g., in conversations);
- follow multi-step directions (e.g., with obstacle courses, working with manipulatives);
- demonstrate knowledge of alphabet (e.g., with Alphabet Bingo, puzzles, name cards);
- listen to a wide variety of literature (i.e., read, read, read!);
- hear and discriminate the sounds of language (e.g., through playing with sound/letter games and name cards);
- begin to decode sounds (e.g., within context of reading or playing with above);
- use pretend writing (e.g., through journal writing or labeling drawings or paintings).

Mathematics Standards in Action

5

Mathematical concepts are an important part of everyday life. Recognizing similarities and differences in size, shape, position, and other characteristics enables us to function more efficiently in daily tasks (setting a table, sorting laundry). Assessing quantities (by number, weight, or volume)

is essential in preparing food or dealing with money. Young children are absorbing mathematical information as they play with objects like sorting boxes, pour and measure sand, help with household chores, and learn to wait their turn (who's first? last?). And we, as adults, must guide them in further understanding by providing them with the vocabulary of mathematics. We identify shapes for them. We talk about the positions of objects. We count out loud and explain first, second, and third. We give structure to the passage of time, and words to identify more or less. We introduce them to addition and subtraction as we add or take away items or people in various situations. We

give names to numerals and relate them to the quantities they represent. We help them learn to represent mathematical findings in charts and graphs.

In this chapter, we have chosen seven standards from different states that cover the range of mathematical early learning standards around the country. We recognize that there are many more ways to address these standards than the ideas we have put forth here. We invite you to think about your classroom and curriculum. How will you address these standards in your program?

Early Learning Standards	Common Practices in an Early Childhood Classroom Where This Standard May Be Addressed

"Show increasing abilities to match, sort, put in a series, and regroup objects according to one or two attributes (i.e., shape, size)"

—*Alabama Performance Standards for 4-year-olds: Alabama's Pre-Kindergarten Initiative Ready for School, Ready to Learn*

Other states with similar standards:
CA, CO, CT, DC, GA, IL, IA, LA, MD, MA, MN, NE, NY, OK, RI, TX, UT

Providing many opportunities for children to work and play with manipulatives (such as puzzles, colored blocks, and collections of objects like buttons or beads) that involve matching, sorting, and grouping

Young children love to work with real objects, trying out different ways of using them, being creative and self-directed in organizing and constructing with them. You can add the idea of matching and sorting to their explorations of manipulatives starting with simple one-on-one matching and leading to more sophisticated sorting by one and two attributes.

	First Steps Toward the Standard:	**Making Progress Toward the Standard:**	**Accomplishing the Standard:**
What the Children Might Show You: *A range of awareness of similarities and differences between objects*	Recognizes the similarities between two objects and can match them consistently	Identifies the difference between objects and can group them by one attribute (such as color or size)	Identifies the difference between several objects and can group them by more than one attribute (such as big red ones and small green ones)
Curriculum and Activities that You Can Plan and Implement for Each Child's Progress Level	• As a child works with puzzles and manipulatives, converse back and forth about the similarities of different pieces. • Working together, do one-on-one matching with small colored cubes or stringing beads for a necklace. • Play matching games like Memory or Shape Bingo. • Encourage children to make up their own matching games for you to try.	• Converse with children about similarities and differences among objects and manipulatives, talking about color, shape, and size differences. • Ask a child if he can find all of the red ones or put all of the round ones in the basket. • Suggest that children use stringing beads to make all yellow necklaces. Or, with pattern blocks, sort out all of the triangles and make a design with them. • Play matching games like Memory or Shape Bingo and encourage more sorting. • Encourage children to make up their own sorting games for you to try.	• Continue to converse with children about similarities and differences among objects and manipulatives, talking about color, shape, size, textures, and more subtle differences. • Ask a child to sort objects by two attributes: Can you find all of the large orange blocks and stack them? • Suggest that children make a necklace with small, round beads or make a design with square and circular pattern blocks. • Play people-sorting games (all boys with tie shoes, or children with belts and blond hair). Let the children be the sorters.

Early Learning Standards

Common Practices in an Early Childhood Classroom Where This Standard May Be Addressed

"Children show interest and curiosity in counting and grouping objects and numbers."

—*Vermont Early Learning Standards: Guiding the Development and Learning of Children Entering Kindergarten*

Other states with similar standards:
CA, CO, CT, DC, GA, IL, IA, LA, MD, MA, MI, MN, NE, NJ, NY, OK, RI, SC, TX, UT

Counting throughout the day in daily activities and routines, in conversations indoors and out

Find as many ways as possible to make counting and numbers a part of every-day activities in the classroom! This can include counting the number of children present and absent, the number of boys and girls, the number of days in the week, the number of places at a table, the number of children in line, the number of blocks in a tower, the number of marks in a painting, the number of buttons on a jacket, the number of steps up the slide, the number of birds at the bird feeder, etc.

Access state standards at www.ccsso.org/ECEAstandards. For information correlating state standards, go to www.nieer.org/standards/statelist.php.

	First Steps Toward the Standard:	**Making Progress Toward the Standard:**	**Accomplishing the Standard:**
What the Children Might Show You: *A range of interest, curiosity, and awareness of quantity*	Shows little interest or curiosity in counting or little awareness or accuracy when identifying quantities	Is beginning to count objects or people with awareness of quantity and one-to-one correspondence in small quantities	Is beginning to count objects or people with awareness of quantity and one-to one-correspondence in larger quantities
Curriculum and Activities that You Can Plan and Implement for Each Child's Progress Level	• As a child works and plays, converse back and forth about the quantities of objects, children, chairs, crackers, etc. • Include counting in daily routines of attendance, snack preparation, washing hands, and choosing learning areas. • Sing or chant finger plays and songs with counting (such as "Three Green and Speckled Frogs"). • Accept the child's level of participation in these activities. Do not force the child to count so that a power struggle develops and the math experience becomes a negative one. • Make counting activities fun parts of every day.	• Continue to converse back and forth about the quantities of objects, children, chairs, crackers, etc., asking children to help you count. Start with small quantities. • Include counting in even more daily routines. • Sing or chant finger plays and songs with counting (such as "Five Little Monkeys"). • Read counting books to large and small groups and individual children or count objects in books read. • Play counting games outdoors: Jump three times. Swing back and forth five times. • Encourage children to count throughout the day.	• Continue to increase the quantities of objects you converse about, sing about, read about, and incorporate in daily routines. • Play movement games that ask children to clap and count, stomp and count. "Simon says, 'Clap two times.'" Increase the quantities as children are able to follow through successfully. • Introduce numerals and help children see the connection between the symbol and the quantity. • Encourage children to count throughout the day to higher and higher quantities.

Early Learning Standards	Common Practices in an Early Childhood Classroom Where This Standard May Be Addressed

"The child will describe simple geometric shapes (circle, triangle, rectangle, and square) and indicate their position in relation to him/herself and to other objects."

—*Virginia Mathematics Foundation Block 4 Geometry*

Other states with similar standards:
CA, CO, CT, DC, GA, IL, IA, LA, MD, MA, MI, MN, NE, NJ, NY, OH, OK, RI, TX, UT

Making geometry and spatial awareness part of the classroom environment, materials, and activities as children work and play and go about their daily routines

Children are exploring the world around them and learning the vocabulary to identify shape names (circle, triangle, square) and their attributes (round, three corners, four even sides) as well as to understand directionality, dimensions, and manipulation of objects in space (up, down, behind, under). You can give them many opportunities to build and construct with blocks and other objects, to create shapes through art materials, to move their own bodies in space, and to learn more about the vocabulary of shapes and directions.

	First Steps Toward the Standard:	Making Progress Toward the Standard:	Accomplishing the Standard:
What the Children Might Show You: An increasing vocabulary for geometric shapes and spatial awareness	Begins to distinguish and name shapes and directions	Distinguishes and names some shapes and directions	Distinguishes and names several shapes and directions
Curriculum and Activities that You Can Plan and Implement for Each Child's Progress Level	• Provide puzzles and manipulatives that include a variety of geometric shapes. • Include a variety of geometric shapes throughout the environment (such as labels on tables and cubbies, on bulletin boards and posters). • As a child works and plays, converse back and forth about the shapes of objects and their placement in space. • Describe a child's actions in terms of directionality: You just went under the bridge. You put that cylinder on top of your tower. • Do not force the child to name shapes or directions so that a power struggle or a negative experience develops.	• Continue to converse back and forth about the shapes of objects and their placement in space as children use manipulatives and play and work in the classroom. Describe their differences and similarities. • Encourage the child to name shapes that she knows or describe the placement of objects or her body in space. Help with vocabulary if necessary. • Play Shape Bingo or I Spy with shapes in the environment. • Point out shapes in clothing, books, artwork, signs, and nature. • Play Simon Says and other movement games using directional words.	• Continue to converse back and forth about the shapes of objects and their placement in space as children use manipulatives and play and work in the classroom. Have the children describe their differences and similarities. • Encourage the child to name shapes that she knows or describe placement of objects or her body in space. • Play Shape Bingo or I Spy with even more shapes in the environment. • Have the children identify shapes in clothing, books, artwork, signs, and nature. • Play Simon Says and other movement games using even more directional words.

Early Learning Standards

Common Practices in an Early Childhood Classroom Where This Standard May Be Addressed

"Number, number sense, and operations standard:

PreK-2 Benchmark: Recognize, classify, compare, and order whole numbers

Prekindergarten Indicator: Compare and order whole numbers up to 5.

Compare sets of equal, more, and fewer and use the language of comparison (e.g., equal, more, and fewer)."

—*Ohio Early Learning Content Standards*

Other states with similar standards:
CA, CO, CT, DC, GA, IL, IA, LA, MD, MA, MI, MN, NE, NJ, NY, OK, RI, SC, TX, UT

Providing opportunities for children to recognize and order numbers up to five and compare quantities as children work and play and go about their daily routines

Preschool children are keenly aware of more and less! Their egocentrism helps them to pay attention to the differences in quantities of food or toys or special privileges. This can be used to teach mathematical understanding not only at snack time or in conflicts over sharing, but also in measuring at the sand and water tables or in cooking and food preparation as well as in working with collections of objects or building with manipulatives or blocks. Adding the symbolic representation of whole numbers one through five helps children make the connection between quantitative writing and actual quantities. Learning about the order of numbers helps build that one-to-one correspondence that is the foundation of our mathematical system.

	First Steps Toward the Standard:	Making Progress Toward the Standard:	Accomplishing the Standard:
What the Children Might Show You: A growing awareness of and vocabulary to describe differences in quantities plus an ability to recognize and order numbers	Shows some awareness or accuracy when comparing quantities and/or little accuracy in naming or ordering whole numbers	Shows more frequent accuracy when comparing quantities but may not describe the differences; accurately names or orders two or three whole numbers	Consistently is accurate when comparing quantities using vocabulary of equal, more, or less and naming and ordering whole numbers one through five
Curriculum and Activities that You Can Plan and Implement for Each Child's Progress Level	• Provide sand, water, or other substances in tubs or a sensory table for children to measure and pour. • As a child works and plays, converse back and forth comparing quantities. • Point out numeric order when counting and ordering objects in everyday activities. • Display numerals in order in meaningful ways (such as on a calendar, on a counting line, on waiting lists or sign-in sheets, etc.). • Do not force the child to use comparative words or order numbers so that a power struggle or a negative experience develops.	• As a child works and plays at the sand table or cooking, converse back and forth comparing quantities. Encourage use of descriptive words "more" and "less." • Have children begin to identify numeric order when counting and ordering objects in everyday activities. Which is first? Second? • Display numerals in order in meaningful ways (such as on a calendar, on a counting line, on waiting lists or sign-in sheets, etc.) and encourage children to point to them as they count with special attention from one to three.	• Continue to provide materials to encourage comparison of quantities and use of the words *more*, *less*, and *equal*. • Encourage identification of numeric order in a variety of activities. What number comes next? • In addition to numerals displayed in meaningful ways, provide numeral puzzles and matching games and, as children work with them, give special focus on ordering numbers one through five. • Make number books using stickers or collage materials with children up to five.

Early Learning Standards	Common Practices in an Early Childhood Classroom Where This Standard May Be Addressed

"Understand the concept of measurement"

—*Wisconsin Model Early Learning Standards*

Other states with similar standards:
CA, CO, CT, DC, GA, IL, IA, LA, MD, MA, MN, NE, NJ, NY, OK, RI, TX, UT

Providing experiences for children as they work, play, and go about their daily routines to observe adults measuring objects and to try out ways of measuring for themselves

As preschool children learn about quantities such as more and less, they are also learning about bigger and smaller, longer and shorter, heavier and lighter. The vocabulary of comparison is also the vocabulary of measurement. Helping children to compare objects, to use nonstandard references of measurement, and to begin to use measurement tools is all part of developing their mathematical understanding.

Access state standards at www.ccsso.org/ECEAstandards. For information correlating state standards, go to www.nieer.org/standards/statelist.php.

	First Steps Toward the Standard:	**Making Progress Toward the Standard:**	**Accomplishing the Standard:**
What the Children Might Show You: A range of interest and awareness of ways to compare and measure the sizes of objects	Shows some awareness or accuracy when comparing the sizes of objects but may not have the vocabulary to describe the differences	Shows more frequent accuracy when comparing the sizes of objects and uses more comparative words (longer, heavier, smaller) in his vocabulary	Consistently uses comparative words when comparing the sizes of objects and begins to use measurement tools (not necessarily with accuracy) such as rulers or yardsticks
Curriculum and Activities that You Can Plan and Implement for Each Child's Progress Level	• Provide many toys for construction and manipulation (large and small blocks, Lego building blocks, connectors, etc.). • As a child works and plays, converse back and forth comparing the sizes of objects. • Model measuring objects one against another or by using a measurement tool in play and in meaningful everyday activities. • Do not force the child to use comparative words or measurement tools so that a power struggle or a negative experience develops.	• As a child works and plays with toys for construction and manipulation, converse back and forth comparing the sizes of objects. Encourage use of descriptive words, "longer, shorter," "heavier, lighter," "largest, smallest," etc. • Continue to model measuring objects in everyday activities. Invite children to help you. • Record the results of measuring on visually attractive graphs: heights of plants as they grow from seeds; heights of the children in the group; weights of pumpkins from the pumpkin farm; etc.	• Continue to provide materials to encourage comparison of sizes and use of comparative words. • Continue to model measuring objects in everyday activities and encourage children to identify opportunities to do so using measurement tools when it makes sense. • Invite children to figure out ways to record the results of their measurement activities. • Introduce vocabulary related to units of measurement that go with the measurement tools used: inches, millimeters, pounds, ounces, etc.

Early Learning Standards	Common Practices in an Early Childhood Classroom Where This Standard May Be Addressed

"Standard 5: Data Analysis—The child will collect and analyze data in a group setting.

2. Develops growing abilities to collect, describe, and record information through a variety of means, including discussion, drawings, maps, charts, and graphs."

—*Oklahoma Pre-Kindergarten Curriculum Guidelines*

Other states with similar standards:
CO, CT, DC, IL, LA, MD, MA, NY, SC, TX, UT

Modeling ways to collect and analyze data and information for children in large and small group discussions and in conversations as children work, play, and go about their daily routines; providing materials and assistance to help children begin to record information that is meaningful to them

Young children are very hands-on. They are learning about the world through their own explorations of materials, observations of events, and imitations of others in their lives. Language becomes more and more a way that they are able to describe and analyze what they are learning. And as adults demonstrate for them ways to record information, they can begin to experiment with drawings, maps, charts, and graphs. But they will always need to have direct experience with what they are representing and have a friendly supportive teacher or parent to guide the way in any recording of information!

Access state standards at www.ccsso.org/ECEAstandards. For information correlating state standards, go to www.nieer.org/standards/statelist.php.

	First Steps Toward the Standard:	**Making Progress Toward the Standard:**	**Accomplishing the Standard:**
What the Children Might Show You: A range of interest, curiosity, and awareness of analyzing and recording data and information	Shows little interest or curiosity in analyzing or recording data—is more hands-on in his approach to tasks	Talks more about experiences and describes what occurred with accuracy but not necessarily detail most of the time	In addition to talking about experiences, begins to use other means to record information or data, such as drawings, maps, charts, or graphs, with adult help
Curriculum and Activities that You Can Plan and Implement for Each Child's Progress Level	• As a child works and plays, converse back and forth, describing what the child is doing and encouraging him to show you what he is up to. • Model ways of being more descriptive and analytical in your conversations. • Introduce some recording techniques to children by making a chart at large or small group time (i.e., "Who's here and who's absent today?" Or take a survey: "Do you like chocolate or white milk better?") • Do not force the child to verbalize or explain so that a power struggle or a negative experience develops.	• As a child works and plays, converse back and forth, encouraging the child to tell you more about what he is up to. • Ask open-ended questions to stimulate the child to be more descriptive and analytical. • Play people-sorting games for children's likes and dislikes. Let children determine the categories and analyze the size of the groups. Introduce recording the results. • Let children use clipboards with paper with two columns labeled "Yes" and "No." Have them determine a question to survey other children on. They can record with a check mark or have children write their names in the columns.	• Continue to converse with children, asking open-ended questions to stimulate them to be descriptive and analytical about whatever they are doing. • Read *Rosie's Walk* and have the children help you make a map that traces everywhere Rosie went. Then make a map of the classroom together. Families could map the child's bedroom for "homework." • Make real-item graphs (on the floor using a shower curtain or large piece of plastic, or paper graphs). Have children bring in fruits for fruit salad and graph the groups of fruit, graph children's types of shoes, etc.

Early Learning Standards	Common Practices in an Early Childhood Classroom Where This Standard May Be Addressed

"Expectation 4: Children develop knowledge of sequence and temporal awareness."

—New Jersey Early Childhood Education Program Expectations: Standards of Quality

Other states with similar standards:
CO, CT, DC, GA, IL, IA, LA, MA, MI, MN, NE, NY, OK, TX, UT

Keeping a consistent and predictable daily routine and giving children plenty of information about any changes coming up; helping children move through transitions from activity to activity by giving five-minute warnings, setting timers, or pointing to clocks and watches; and providing sequencing games and experiences

Young children like predictability! They don't worry about the exact length of time for any activity, but they do like to know what's coming next and what to expect. You can help children learn to trust you by keeping the consistency of the daily routine and alerting them whenever a special event might change that consistency. Beginning to introduce them to ways of timekeeping and giving them the vocabulary to describe time appropriately will help them develop temporal awareness. Also, providing them with sequencing cards and games and having discussions about logical next steps in a sequence will help their thinking skills.

	First Steps Toward the Standard:	Making Progress Toward the Standard:	Accomplishing the Standard:
What the Children Might Show You: A growing awareness of time and the ability to sequence	Shows some awareness or accuracy when talking about times of day with little accuracy in sequencing events	Uses some correct vocabulary to describe the times of day with some accuracy in sequencing events	Uses correct vocabulary more frequently to describe time and begins to show interest in clocks, watches, and timers, and accurately sequences events with up to three steps
Curriculum and Activities that You Can Plan and Implement for Each Child's Progress Level	• As a child works and plays, converse back and forth about different times of day, upcoming activities, and the sequence of events. • Post the daily routine for the children, using drawings or photos to identify the day's activities. Discuss each day. • Give plenty of notice about changes in the routine or upcoming transitions to other activities. Use clear signals or timers that the children can understand. • If a child inaccurately talks about today or yesterday, do not correct her, but do model the correct language back in a naturalistic conversation.	• As a child works and plays encourage her to talk about different times of day, upcoming activities, and the sequence of events. • Have a special "What's next?" helper who uses the posted daily routine to announce the next activity at transition times. • Have a child set the timer for upcoming transitions to other activities. • Introduce children to the features of clocks and watches and refer to them throughout the day (e.g., "When the big hand is on the five, we'll clean up."). • Provide sequencing games and puzzles.	• Continue to converse with children about times of day and sequences of events, encouraging them to predict what's coming next. • Refer to the clock more frequently when talking about time, describing how you read the placement of the hands. • Provide sequencing games and puzzles that include at least three steps (e.g., the hatching of an egg or from caterpillar to butterfly). • Give directions in sequence and make a game of remembering and following them correctly. Let children take the lead (Simons Says with three steps!).

Math Standards in Preschool Learning Areas

Blocks

Children can

- show increasing abilities to match, sort, put in a series, and regroup objects according to one or two attributes (e.g., shape, size);
- show interest and curiosity in counting and grouping objects and numbers;
- describe simple geometric shapes;
- understand the concept of measurement.

As children build and construct, they are continually matching, sorting, and grouping different sizes and shapes of blocks. You can encourage them to count the blocks in their tower or count the number of square blocks they used to make their road. You can also describe the shapes of their blocks and encourage them to make shapes in their constructions. Identifying which blocks are longer or shorter and measuring them using a smaller block or a ruler can also extend block play mathematically.

Dramatic Play

Children can

- show increasing abilities to match, sort, put in a series, and regroup objects according to one or two attributes (e.g., shape, size)
- show interest and curiosity in counting and grouping objects and numbers;
- develop knowledge of sequence and temporal awareness.

In acting out family life and other life experiences, children are sorting and grouping the materials necessary to pretend cook or set the table. They may match all of the red plates or sort all of the plastic fruit into a bowl. You can encourage them to count how many people are at the table and set the table using one-to-one correspondence (one plate, one fork, one napkin for each person). Describing sequences of family routines and times of day for family events can help with understanding of sequence and time.

Manipulatives

Children can

- show increasing abilities to match, sort, put in a series, and regroup objects according to one or two attributes (e.g., shape, size);
- show interest and curiosity in counting and grouping objects and numbers;
- describe simple geometric shapes;

- recognize, classify, compare, and order whole numbers;
- use the language of comparison (e.g., equal, more, and less).

Many manipulatives and puzzles provide children with opportunities to match, sort, categorize, count, group, and compare. Numeral puzzles and number matching games can help children recognize and order numbers.

Art Area

Children can

- describe simple geometric shapes;
- understand the concept of measurement;
- develop knowledge of sequence and temporal awareness.

As children create with a variety of art materials, they may identify geometric shapes, measure and compare sizes of playdough or length of painted lines, and describe the sequence of actions they took to make their creation.

Math Standards Imbedded in Projects That Follow Upon Children's Interests

Many projects include the need for mathematical analysis and documentation. A study of balls may include comparing sizes, sorting by color or material, and graphing or charting the results. Counting, numeric representation, data analysis, and measurement can all be incorporated into a number of topics, discussions, and documentation.

Math Standards That Can Be Imbedded in Large Group Times

Children can

- show increasing abilities to match and sort (e.g., with people sorting);
- show interest and curiosity in counting (e.g., in taking attendance);
- develop knowledge of sequence and temporal awareness (e.g., when reviewing the daily routine).

Math Standards That Can Be Imbedded in Small Group Work

Skills such as matching, sorting, counting, grouping, numbers, measurement, and data analysis can be developed through working with manipulatives and games, graphing and record keeping, reading counting stories and books, making number books, creating patterns, and cooking activities.

Science Standards in Action

6

Young children are investigators, wondering how things work and what will happen next. They experiment in order to learn more about all aspects of their world. Their innate curiosity and joy in discovery is one of the reasons working with them is so rewarding to us as early educators. Seeing the lightbulb go off—the understanding and delight in making something happen and the joy in doing it again—is part of working with preschoolers. We can plan many different ways to capitalize on the inquisitiveness of children and weave in early learning standards in the physical and earth sciences as well. Since the children are exploring through their senses, we can provide opportunities for them to experience many varied sensory experiences. We can encourage their risk taking and welcome their questioning. They may not always understand the scientific principles involved, but they most certainly observe the attraction of a magnet with a metal or the sinking or floating of an object in water. We can expose them to chemical changes as substances are heated or mixed and invite them to describe what they have seen. We can encourage them to make predictions and hypothesize, following the true scientific method as they explore and use scientific tools to better understand their world.

In this chapter, we have chosen five standards from different states that cover the range of scientific early learning standards around the country. We recognize that there are many more ways to address these standards than the ideas we have put forth here. We invite you to think about your classroom and curriculum. How will you address these standards in your program?

Early Learning Standards

Common Practices in an Early Childhood Classroom Where This Standard May Be Addressed

"Standard: Demonstrate understanding of the process of scientific inquiry

S.C. 1.1: Show curiosity by asking questions and seeking information"

—*Pennsylvania Early Learning Standards for Pre-Kindergarten*

Other states with similar standards:
CA, CO, CT, DC, GA, IL, IN, LA, MD, MA, MN, NJ, NY, OH, OK, RI, TX, UT

Providing a variety of enticing materials, setting up scientific experiments for children to try, and welcoming children's questions are ways to stimulate their natural curiosity

You know young children are inquisitive, so you set up your classroom environment so that they can explore and try out many different things and figure out how they work. You ask open-ended questions such as "What do you think will happen if you . . .?" and set up experiments for children to try out, welcoming their predictions and helping them determine if their hypotheses were supported by the results. You continually challenge their thinking and help them find ways to seek new information.

Access state standards at www.ccsso.org/ECEAstandards. For information correlating state standards, go to www.nieer.org/standards/statelist.php.

	First Steps Toward the Standard:	Making Progress Toward the Standard:	Accomplishing the Standard:
What the Children Might Show You: A developing interest in figuring things out for themselves	Tries out various materials through more trial and error than with intent and purpose without asking many questions	Responds to teacher suggestions and open-ended questions to try other ways of using materials or changing results and may ask questions	Initiates own efforts to try other ways of using materials or changing results and asks many questions
Curriculum and Activities that You Can Plan and Implement for Each Child's Progress Level	• As a child works and plays, converse back and forth about ways he is using materials and the results that occur. • Provide a variety of materials and experiences for exploration and allow enough time for children to really get involved. • Ask open-ended questions as children explore. • Invite children to join you in simple experiments in which they can participate in a hands-on way (e.g., mixing baking soda and vinegar and feeling the bubbles, mixing colors, painting with water outdoors and watching it dry). • Welcome children's questions and challenge their thinking.	• As a child works and plays, converse back and forth and encourage him to describe his use of materials and the results. • Follow up on children's explorations by asking them to verbally review what they did and what they noticed. • As you ask open-ended questions, encourage children to consider new ways of using materials. • Welcome children's questions; answer those you can, and demonstrate how you use resources such as books, the Internet, or specialists to gain information. • Provide materials and suggestions so that children can extend their own investigations.	• Continue to engage children in conversations and encourage them to describe what they are doing and the results. • Follow up on children's explorations by having them represent the process and results through a drawing, journal dictation, or photo record. •Encourage children to ask open-ended questions of each other. • Conduct some longer-term experiments (growing seeds in differing light conditions, growing mold on bread) and keep ongoing documentation. • Help children use resources to investigate and seek information.

Early Learning Standards

Common Practices in an Early Childhood Classroom Where This Standard May Be Addressed

"Physical Science: Explores physical properties of objects and materials.

Indicator Examples:

2. Uses one or more senses to observe the physical world."

—Missouri Pre-K Standards

Other states with similar standards:
CA, DC, GA, IL, IN, LA, MD, MA, MN, NJ, OH, OK, RI, TX, UT

Providing as many opportunities as possible for children to explore the world around them using all of their senses: sight, hearing, touch, smell, and taste

Humans learn about their world through their senses, and young children most of all! You know that they need to touch and manipulate materials rather than just look at them in order to truly figure out how they work. You've seen how sensitive they can be to new smells or tastes and how they respond to unfamiliar sounds. You can provide experiences and add verbal explanations and descriptions to help them understand how the physical world works as they feel different textures, as they prepare and eat new foods, as they listen and identify new sounds and styles of music. You can take advantage of their curiosity and sensory nature and help them to be investigative scientists, discovering all that they can about the world around them.

	First Steps Toward the Standard:	**Making Progress Toward the Standard:**	**Accomplishing the Standard:**
What the Children Might Show You: A use of more senses to observe and explore the world and willingness to touch new materials and try new tastes	Uses obvious sensory information to explore the world, reacting more physically than verbally, and may be resistant to try something new	Begins to use more senses to explore the world (not just through the obvious), making some simple comments describing sensory experiences and showing less resistance to new experiences	Uses multiple senses to explore the world and makes more detailed comments describing sensory experiences and showing less resistance to new experiences
Curriculum and Activities that You Can Plan and Implement for Each Child's Progress Level	• As a child works and plays, converse back and forth about clearly observable visual cues, sounds, textures, smells, and tastes modeling use of appropriate and descriptive vocabulary. • Provide materials and experiences that stimulate children's sensory exploration (e.g., sand, water, shaving cream, etc., in sensory table; smelling jars and cooking activities; colorful and interesting art materials, books, and puzzles; recordings of different styles of music). • Talk about how we use our senses.	• As a child works and plays, converse back and forth and encourage use of words to describe colors, sounds, textures, smells, and tastes. • Help children compare and contrast sensory characteristics of a variety of materials. Go on "hunts" around the room for something that looks, sounds, feels, or smells the same. • Provide safe ways for children to try something new (e.g., painting with a wooden stick instead of fingers, wearing plastic gloves to work with shaving cream, taking one small taste of a new food).	• Continue to engage children in conversations and encourage them to describe sensory experiences. • Provide experiences that require children to use multiple senses (e.g., cooking for seeing changes and smelling and tasting the results!). • Make audiotapes of familiar sounds (indoors and out) and children's voices to listen to and identify the source. • Identify textures and smells in natural objects. • Play tasting games and play with a touch and feel box.

Early Learning Standards	Common Practices in an Early Childhood Classroom Where This Standard May Be Addressed

"Science

Standard: Understands basic concepts of scientific inquiry

Rubric: Uses tools to gather information (e.g., magnifying lens, eyedropper, audiocassettes)"

—*Colorado Building Blocks to Colorado's Content Standards*

Other states with similar standards:
CT, DC, GA, IL, IN, MA, MN, OH, RI, TX, UT

Setting up a science area where magnifying lenses, balance scales, prisms, binoculars, audiocassettes, and other tools are available to use for exploration of the classroom and a variety of items from nature

Young children are scientists at heart, wanting to explore and take in information. You recognize their innate curiosity and provide tools for them to gather information about the world in new ways. You guide their use of these tools and describe for them what they are seeing and experiencing. They may not always understand the scientific principles involved even though they may ask many questions. You are building the foundation for their understanding at later ages.

Access state standards at www.ccsso.org/ECEAstandards. For information correlating state standards, go to www.nieer.org/standards/statelist.php.

	First Steps Toward the Standard:	Making Progress Toward the Standard:	Accomplishing the Standard:
What the Children Might Show You: A developing interest in the purposes of various scientific tools and in the results observed when using them	Plays with the tools for a limited time period without much interest in their purpose or the results observed when using them	Shows more interest in the purpose of various scientific tools and the results observed when using them	Uses at least one scientific tool specifically for its intended purpose and comments on the results observed when using it
Curriculum and Activities that You Can Plan and Implement for Each Child's Progress Level	• Set up a science area with a selection of tools available (e.g., magnifying glass, balance scale, prism, kaleidoscope, plastic thermometers, audiocassettes, stethoscopes, binoculars, magnets, etc.). Change periodically. • Demonstrate ways to use these tools to gain information, and model use of descriptive vocabulary to discuss the results observed. • Encourage children to try tools out on a variety of classroom items and items from nature.	• As a child works and plays at the science area, converse back and forth and encourage use of words to describe what she is doing and seeing. • Bring the tools to other areas of the classroom or outdoors to investigate and gather information (e.g., use the magnifying glass to explore the carpet, the floor, wooden and plastic blocks, textures of fabrics, tree trunks, etc.). • Help children record their findings through drawings or science journals.	• Continue to engage children in conversations and encourage them to describe their experiences with these tools. • Read books about scientists and their use of tools to help them in their work. • Encourage children to identify which tool would be most appropriate for specific situations and to follow through on their own inquiries by using the appropriate tool. • Help children record their findings through drawings, written descriptions, and photo documentation.

Early Learning Standards

Common Practices in an Early Childhood Classroom Where This Standard May Be Addressed

"Life Science

Component Learning Expectations: Recognizes that living things are made up of parts

Performance Indicators: Begins to make comparisons among living things, such as flowers, insects, and animals."

—*Tennessee Early Childhood Early Learning Developmental Standards*

Other states with similar standards:
DC, GA, IL, IN, LA, MA, MI, NJ, NY, OH, OK, RI, TX, UT

Giving children many experiences with living things helps them see the differences between plants, insects, animals, and humans

Young children are fascinated with living things in their world, whether it be a frisky puppy, a flower in bloom, or a bug crawling up a tree trunk. You recognize this and include plants and natural materials in your classroom environment. You have some form of classroom pets and point out any animals, insects, or birds in the school neighborhood. You take children on field trips to see farm or zoo animals up close. You plan visits to apple orchards, pumpkin patches, or botanical gardens so that children can learn more about growing things. You provide books, posters, videos, and manipulative replicas so that they can learn more about the life cycles of plants and the vast array of creatures on the earth.

Access state standards at www.ccsso.org/ECEAstandards. For information correlating state standards, go to www.nieer.org/standards/statelist.php.

	First Steps Toward the Standard:	**Making Progress Toward the Standard:**	**Accomplishing the Standard:**
What the Children Might Show You: A developing interest in and ability to describe different kinds of living things	Shows some interest and uses simple vocabulary when describing living things	Shows more interest and uses more descriptive words when describing living things	Begins to verbally compare and contrast characteristics of living things with some accuracy

Curriculum and Activities that You Can Plan and Implement for Each Child's Progress Level			

First Steps Toward the Standard:

- As a child works and plays, converse back and forth about living plants and animals modeling use of descriptive vocabulary.

- Include plants and classroom pets as part of the room environment. Have children help in the care of them.

- Point out any living things in the indoor or outdoor school environment. Discuss characteristics and what they need to grow and thrive.

- Provide books, posters, and videos about plants and animals.

- Include manipulative replicas of many kinds of animals for children to play with in the block and manipulatives area.

Making Progress Toward the Standard:

- As a child works and plays, converse back and forth and encourage use of words to describe living plants and animals.

- As children help care for classroom pets and plants, have them describe what they are learning about them.

- Go on insect hunts and bird-watching walks outdoors. Follow up by recording what children saw and noticed.

- Plant seeds and watch them grow. Have children describe the changes they are noticing. Document with photos and drawings.

- Make a class graph of family pets. Compare and contrast similarities and differences.

Accomplishing the Standard:

- Continue to engage children in conversations and encourage them to describe living plants and animals, comparing and contrasting their characteristics.

- In response to children's fascination with specific animals, provide books, posters, videos, and special visitors to help them study that animal in more depth. Document what children are learning about that animal.

- Plant bulbs or a vegetable garden, tend to them, and document their growth.

- Visit a zoo, farm, aquarium, botanical garden, orchard, etc., and follow up with group discussions and class books.

Early Learning Standards	Common Practices in an Early Childhood Classroom Where This Standard May Be Addressed

"**F. THE EARTH: Students will gain knowledge about the earth and the processes that change it.**

ELEMENTARY GRADES Pre-K–2 students will be able to:

Describe the way weather changes.

Analyze the relationships between observable weather patterns and the cycling of the seasons.

Observe changes that are caused by water, snow, wind, and ice."

—*Maine Learning Results*

Other states with similar standards:
CO, DC, GA, IL, IN, LA, MA, NY, OH, OK, TX, UT

Daily discussions about the weather and the noticeable aspects of the changing of the seasons in large and small groups as well as in individual conversations around going outside, getting ready to go home, dressing, etc.

Young children are interested in the world around them. You can capitalize on their fascination with observable changes in weather conditions and seasonal changes. By doing so, you will stimulate their observation skills, develop their descriptive vocabulary, help them draw conclusions about appropriate clothing and activities, and give them more information about the predictability of seasonal change and the unpredictability of the weather!

Access state standards at www.ccsso.org/ECEAstandards. For information correlating state standards, go to www.nieer.org/standards/statelist.php.

	First Steps Toward the Standard:	Making Progress Toward the Standard:	Accomplishing the Standard:
What the Children Might Show You: A developing awareness of and ability to describe different kinds of weather and seasons	Shows some awareness and uses simple vocabulary when describing the weather or identifying seasonal changes	Shows more awareness and uses more descriptive words when describing the weather or identifying seasonal changes	Consistently notices the weather when asked and uses more descriptive words when describing the weather or identifying seasonal changes
Curriculum and Activities that You Can Plan and Implement for Each Child's Progress Level	• As a child arrives or departs, works and plays, converse back and forth about the daily weather. • Point out clearly observable weather-related and seasonal characteristics as children prepare for and play outside, modeling use of appropriate and descriptive vocabulary. • Make identifying weather part of the daily routine in some way. • Read weather-related and seasonal books at large and small group times. • Adopt a tree on the school property and visit it periodically in different seasons to note its changes.	• As a child arrives or departs, works and plays, converse back and forth about the daily weather. Encourage use of descriptive words such as "sunny," "cloudy," "rainy," "hot," and "cold." • Have children begin to identify clearly observable weather-related and seasonal characteristics as children prepare for and play outside. • Assign a weather helper who displays recognizable symbols for the weather and may describe the weather to the group. • Go on walks and collect nature items for seasonal collages. Compare leaves in different seasons. Note flowers and changes in temperatures outdoors.	• Continue to engage children in conversations and encourage identification of weather conditions and seasonal changes. • Have the weather helper describe and record the weather in an ongoing weather journal or poster. • Read weather-related and seasonal books and follow up by making related class books. • Provide seasonal sorting puzzles and play sorting games with outdoor clothing for different seasons. • Go on field trips at different times of year. Follow up with group documentation about what was observed in nature.

Science Standards in Preschool Learning Areas

Blocks

Children can

- show curiosity by asking questions and seeking information;

- use one or more senses to observe the physical world;

- use tools to gather information (e.g., magnifying lens, eye-dropper, audiocassettes).

As children build and construct, they use their senses to figure out the weight, length, and shapes of the blocks and place them in a way that will work with gravity most successfully. Encourage them to describe their building strategies and ask open-ended questions to stimulate their thinking and curiosity. They can use magnifying glasses to look more closely at the makeup of differing blocks, weighing blocks in a balance or seeing if any blocks attract a magnet.

Dramatic Play

Children can

- begin to make comparisons among living things, such as flowers, insects, and animals;

- build weather-related themes into their play (e.g., rain, snow, and wind).

Many children love to act out animals and do so with accuracy representing their specific characteristics. You can encourage them to investigate more fully in books and videos how an animal moves, cares for its young, makes sounds, feeds itself, and takes shelter.

Manipulatives

Children can

- use one or more senses to observe the physical world;

- begin to make comparisons among living things, such as flowers, insects, and animals;

- describe and analyze weather changes.

You can provide puzzles and games that reflect weather and seasonal changes and that show sequences of life cycles (e.g., caterpillar to butterfly). Animal and plant lotto games and animal and insect counters can all stimulate discussions and develop vocabulary about living things. Many manipulatives have unique textures, colors, and shapes that can all be part of sensory explorations as well.

Science and Cooking Areas

Children can

- show curiosity by asking questions and seeking information;

- use one or more senses to observe the physical world;

- begin to make comparisons among living things, such as flowers, insects, and animals;

- use tools to gather information (e.g., magnifying lens, eyedropper, audiocassettes).

You can provide a specific science area for use of a variety of scientific tools and for conducting experiments such as growing seeds, identifying smells or tastes, or observing natural phenomena such as the hatching of chicks or butterflies. Cooking activities are ripe with opportunities to use the senses and to observe chemical reactions and changes.

Science Standards Imbedded in Projects That Follow Upon Children's Interests

Many projects include the need for scientific investigation. The content of many children's interests is scientific in nature. They can put forth hypotheses and test them out. You can document for them or help them do so in drawings, constructions, and photos as they investigate a topic such as birds, water, gardening, or fish.

Science Standards That Can Be Imbedded in Large Group Times

All of the science standards identified in this chapter can be imbedded in group time activities. Daily weather reports, class discussions of seasonal changes, group experiments with or without special scientific tools, and reading beautiful photographic books about living things all can be a regular part of large group times.

Science Standards That Can Be Imbedded in Small Group Work

Experiments and cooking activities, as well as use of special tools (such as audiocassette players, binoculars, or microscopes) are best done in smaller groups because they require more close adult supervision. Following up on field trips to the zoo or aquarium with small group story-writing and documentation allows children to reflect on their experiences with the animals or fish that were seen.

Social Studies Standards in Action

7

Young children are eager to learn about the people and places in their world. They start from a very egocentric perspective and show great interest in themselves and their families. From there, they move outward toward the parts of their community with which they come into direct contact:

their neighborhood, their school or child care program, their religious community, the stores and services with which they are familiar (the fire station, the library, the grocery store). Only as they learn to understand and feel safe in their immediate communities that relate directly to their more self-centered needs and interests can they move outward and take in more information about the world at large. As early educators, we can build upon their interest in the people and places in their direct experience and use that as the launching point to introduce them to other places, other traditions, and other cultures.

Throughout all of our work with them in the social studies area, we are modeling acceptance and openness to differences as well as the unifying aspects of humanity.

In this chapter, we have chosen five standards from different states that cover the range of early learning standards in the area of social studies from around the country. We recognize that there are many more ways to address these standards than the ideas we have put forth here. We invite you to think about your classroom and curriculum. How will you address these standards in your program?

Early Learning Standards

Common Practices in an Early Childhood Classroom Where This Standard May Be Addressed

"Cognitive Development and General Knowledge

Subdomain V.C.: Social Studies

People, Past and Present
1. Identifies similarities and differences in personal and family characteristics"

—*Florida Four Year Olds Performance Standards*

Other states with similar standards:
CA, CO, CT, DC, IL, IA, LA, MD, MA, MI, MN, NE, NJ, NY, OK, RI, TX, UT

Helping children see their own uniqueness and the unique characteristics of others will build their sense of self and their sense of acceptance of other people

You do much with young children to help them learn about themselves. You do "All about Me" activities that ask them to identify distinguishing characteristics about their appearance, their family members, their interests, and their experiences. You help them develop a positive sense of self and to show acceptance and kindness toward others. You provide materials that reflect each child's culture and background as well as ones that give them a window on the world of different cultures and backgrounds. All of these steps will lead them to be more productive citizens of the world at large.

	First Steps Toward the Standard:	**Making Progress Toward the Standard:**	**Accomplishing the Standard:**
What the Children Might Show You: Identification of a range of similar and different characteristics about themselves and others	Identifies one characteristic about self in common with another child (e.g., "We're both boys.")	Identifies one characteristic in common and one that is different from another child (e.g., "We're both boys but he's taller.")	Identifies more than one characteristic in common or more than one that is different from other children
Curriculum and Activities that You Can Plan and Implement for Each Child's Progress Level	• As a child works and plays, converse back and forth about his personal characteristics and those of others: gender, hair and eye color, family members, interests. • Display photos of the children and their families on bulletin boards, in photo journals about the class, on cubbies, on attendance and helper boards. Talk about the photos and the similarities and differences. • Trace children's bodies on large sheets of paper for them to paint or color. Discuss and display. • Use common characteristics to sort children for transitions or for people-sorting games.	• As a child works and plays, converse back and forth, encouraging him to talk about his personal characteristics and those of others. • Make "All About Me" books for children to dictate traits about themselves with drawings or photos to accompany dictations. • Measure children's heights, shoe sizes, or handprints. Compare and display on graphs or documentation boards. • Provide multi-ethnic baby dolls, posters, books, etc., to reflect the children and provide examples of different cultures. • Model acceptance of differences.	• Continue to engage children in conversations and encourage discussion of personal characteristics and those of others. • Provide multi-ethnic baby dolls, posters, books, music, etc., to reflect the children's families and provide examples of different cultures. • Provide skin color crayons, paints, and construction paper and encourage children to make portraits that reflect them and their friends. • Model acceptance and help children talk through any situations where inappropriate comments are made.

Early Learning Standards

Common Practices in an Early Childhood Classroom Where This Standard May Be Addressed

"Cognitive Development:
Social Connections

Widely Held Expectations

Children begin to:
• Participate as a member of the group in a democratic classroom community."

—*North Carolina Early Learning Standards*

Other states with similar standards:
CT, DC, GA, IL, LA, MD, MA, MN, NJ, NY, OK, RI, TX, UT

Guiding children to take responsibility for the successful and peaceful functioning of the classroom community builds their understanding of democracy and begins the process of welcoming them as citizens of the larger society

You spend much time helping children learn to get along in the group, sharing materials, taking turns, getting help when needed, using kind and considerate words and actions, and vocalizing their feelings, needs, and opinions. All of this is building their capabilities as responsible, independent members of the learning community you are creating. Although you may not see the fully responsible people they will become, you can rest assured that your efforts at helping them make tiny steps toward responsibility and independence will serve as the foundation upon which they will build their own sense of being a citizen in a democracy.

Access state standards at www.ccsso.org/ECEAstandards. For information correlating state standards, go to www.nieer.org/standards/statelist.php.

	First Steps Toward the Standard:	Making Progress Toward the Standard:	Accomplishing the Standard:
What the Children Might Show You: A developing awareness of ways to get along in a community	Begins to take steps to share, take turns, or follow classroom rules. Some impulsive, selfish behavior still evident.	More frequently shares, takes turns, and follows classroom rules showing concern for other children	Often shares, takes turns, follows classroom rules, shows concern, and makes suggestions for problem solving within the community
Curriculum and Activities that You Can Plan and Implement for Each Child's Progress Level	• As children work and play, make comments about ways you see sharing, caring, and thoughtfulness in action. • Calmly intervene when children have conflicts and model ways to talk through problems, compromise, and come to resolution. • Decide on simple, positively phrased classroom rules and discuss frequently with the children. (e.g., "We take care of ourselves. We take care of each other. And we take care of our school.") • Give children opportunities to make choices and decisions about activities. Make the choices clear.	• As children work and play, make comments about ways you see sharing, caring, and thoughtfulness in action and encourage children to do the same. • Calmly intervene when children have conflicts and encourage them to talk through problems, compromise, and come to resolution. Be prepared to help. • Encourage children to verbalize classroom rules and help each other remember them. Have group discussions about incidents that occur and invite children's opinions and thoughts. • Give children opportunities to make choices and decisions about activities. Make the choices clear.	• Continue to engage children in conversations and encourage identification discussion of personal characteristics and those of others. • Set up a Peace Table or conflict resolution location. Be prepared to help children make good use of their negotiation skills. • Invite children to contribute ideas regarding rules and procedures and problems that arise around them. Try out some of their suggestions and follow through to evaluate their success. • Set up opportunities for children to vote on issues or ideas. • Do a class community project.

Early Learning Standards

"**5. Early Learning Expectation:**
Children increase their understanding about how basic economic concepts relate to their lives.

Children typically:
1. Can talk about some of the workers and services in their community.
2. Can talk about some of the ways people earn a living.
3. Begin to understand that people pay for things with a representation of money (e.g., currency, checks, debit cards, credit cards).
4. Make simple choices about how to spend money."

—*Michigan Early Learning Expectations for Three- and Four-Year-Old Children*

Other states with similar standards:
DC, IL, LA, MD, MA, MN, NJ, OK, TX

Common Practices in an Early Childhood Classroom Where This Standard May Be Addressed

Introducing children to different types of jobs and community workers helps them begin to see how basic economics relate to their lives. Providing dramatic play opportunities and materials for them to imitate familiar jobs and roles, bringing in police officers or firefighters to visit the classroom, or going on field trips to grocery stores or other workplaces helps children expand their thinking about workers in the community.

Young children love to imitate the adults in their lives and learn much by doing so. You provide dress-up clothes that reflect a number of adult roles, including those of workers in various occupations. Community helpers such as firefighters and police officers appear to be superheroes to the children. Even their love of you, as teacher, shows up in their dramatic play as they read to invisible kids and boss them around in ways you are sure you never do! By helping children think more about and role-play various occupations, you are introducing them to the market economy and giving them an opportunity to imitate and explore aspects of work and money.

	First Steps Toward the Standard:	**Making Progress Toward the Standard:**	**Accomplishing the Standard:**
What the Children Might Show You: An increasing interest and accuracy in depicting adult occupations in play and discussions	Imitates some adult occupations simply (e.g., a firefighter putting out a fire)	Adds more details to role playing of occupations, asking questions about specifics in play and discussions	Role plays and discussions of occupations are more extensive and detailed, including information learned from teacher input, books, visitors, and field trips
Curriculum and Activities that You Can Plan and Implement for Each Child's Progress Level	• As children act out adult occupations, make comments about other things involved in those roles. • Provide a variety of hats, uniforms, and other dress-up items to represent a variety of occupations. • Read stories about community helpers and adult occupations. • Invite parents and family members to visit and talk about their jobs. Invite other community members (a police officer, the school nurse) to visit the classroom.	• As children act out adult occupations, make comments about other things involved in those roles and encourage them to add more details in their play. • Encourage children to be creative in adding items to the dress-up area to expand their role plays. • Follow up stories and visitors with related group discussions, role plays, and drawings about various jobs. • Take children on field trips to visit workplaces in the community.	• Continue to engage children in conversations and encourage identification of aspects of occupational roles. • Introduce the concept of money where appropriate in the dramatic play (e.g., grocery store or restaurant). • Add items seen on field trips to extend the play (e.g., a city map for the fire station, pricing stickers for the store, menus and order pads for the restaurant). • Follow up field trips with discussions, group murals, and experience stories. • Write "When I Grow Up, I Want to Be . . ." class book.

Early Learning Standards	Common Practices in an Early Childhood Classroom Where This Standard May Be Addressed

"Geography: Develop an understanding of location, place, relationships within places, movement, and region
Developmental Profile Indicators: PK-CSS-G3
Develop awareness of the world around them"

—*The Louisiana Standards for Programs Serving Four-Year-Old Children*

Other states with similar standards:
CO, DC, IL, MA, MI, MN, NJ, OK, TX

Discussing locations, places, and regions with children within the realm of their personal experiences; reading books about other places; and looking at maps of local community areas as well as a globe of the earth helps children begin to develop geographic awareness

You help children begin to develop a sense of place by engaging them in discussions about their home and community and their personal travels. You expose them to the tools used to explore geographic locations (maps and globes) and bring in books and resources to give them more information about faraway places that have meaning or hold interest for them. You are always careful to keep it relevant and meaningful to the children's experiences!

	First Steps Toward the Standard:	**Making Progress Toward the Standard:**	**Accomplishing the Standard:**
What the Children Might Show You: A developing awareness of the world around them	Makes some comments about the location of home and school within her community	Makes comments about the location of home, school, and community within the region	Makes comments about her own region and shows interest in learning about other regions on earth
Curriculum and Activities that You Can Plan and Implement for Each Child's Progress Level	• As children arrive, work, and play, converse with them about distinctions between home and school, routes and modes of transportation taken, location in community, etc. • Introduce children to the layout of your center or school. Take them on a walk and learn the locations of the kitchen, office, etc. • Read the book *Rosie's Walk* and reenact her movements. Make maps to trace her path. • Go on a neighborhood walk and note places of interest. Follow up by charting what was seen and creating a map of the walk. • Locate children's home addresses on a city map and mark with flags or stickers. • Invite children to share personal travel experiences.	• As children arrive, work, and play, converse with them and encourage their comments about distinctions between home and school, routes and modes of transportation taken, location in community, etc. • Introduce children to the layout of your center or school. After taking a walk, map the locations of the kitchen, office, etc., on a chart. • Make up a class address and phone book to accompany a city map. Discuss who lives close to whom. • Provide puzzles of the U.S. and a globe of the earth. • In group discussions about personal travels include references to country or state.	• Continue to engage children in conversations and encourage identification of information about home and school locations. Set up arrival graphs for attendance with children's photos and/or names for them to place at home or school. Graph modes of transport. • Encourage children to map the layout of your center or school with blocks. • Write a letter to each family and go on a field trip to the post office and mail them. Trace their path through the city on a map. • Read stories about other parts of the country and world that reflect the interests and experiences of the children. • Locate children's travels on a U.S. map or globe.

Early Learning Standards	Common Practices in an Early Childhood Classroom Where This Standard May Be Addressed

"Social Studies Standard 2: Appreciate their own and other cultures (cultural anthropology)"

—*Hawai'i Preschool Content Standards: Curriculum Guidelines for Programs for Four-Year-Olds*

Other states with similar standards:
CA, CO, CT, DC, IL, IA, LA, MD, MA, MI, MN, NE, NJ, NY, OK, RI, TX, UT

Providing opportunities for children and their families to share more about their cultural backgrounds and including materials in the environment to reflect various aspects of different cultures validates children's personal experiences and broadens their awareness of others

You help children recognize their own family traditions by reflecting their cultures in the materials in your classroom and by welcoming their family members to share celebrations, foods, music, and daily life experiences with the whole class. You respond to children's interests in other cultures by providing additional books, posters, recordings, videos, special visitors, and field trips to learn more about the cultures of the world. Throughout, you are sensitive to represent the daily lives of other peoples instead of just focusing on a "tourist curriculum" approach and are constantly helping children to share the common humanity of all peoples of the earth.

Access state standards at www.ccsso.org/ECEAstandards. For information correlating state standards, go to www.nieer.org/standards/statelist.php.

	First Steps Toward the Standard:	Making Progress Toward the Standard:	Accomplishing the Standard:
What the Children Might Show You: A developing appreciation of their own and others' cultures and traditions	Talks about some of his own family traditions and may incorporate into play	Talks about some of his own family traditions and shows interest in those of other children's families and may incorporate into play	Talks about various families' traditions and incorporates into play and shows interest in other cultures as well
Curriculum and Activities that You Can Plan and Implement for Each Child's Progress Level	• As children work and play, converse with children about their own family structures and cultural traditions. • Survey family members about their cultural backgrounds and traditions so that you are well informed. • Provide dramatic play materials, posters, and books that reflect the cultures of the children in your class. • Invite family members to visit and share more about family traditions. • Model acceptance and interest in differing traditions and cultural traits.	• As children arrive, work, and play, converse with children and encourage their comments about their own family structures and cultural traditions. • Invite children and families to contribute items to the classroom that reflect their backgrounds. • Have a class potluck dinner with various types of foods for tasting, music to listen to, and new games to try. • Include creative works, foods, and music from a variety of cultures on a regular basis in the classroom (not necessarily tied to any special holidays). • Portray different cultures in daily life as well as in ceremonial dress for special celebrations.	• Continue to engage children in conversations and respond to their questions and interest in cultural traditions. • Encourage children's dramatic play and creative expressions to accurately reflect various cultural traditions. • Read stories in different languages or read the same fable from several different cultural perspectives. • Visit a cultural or ethnic museum or invite special visitors to share and expand the range of cultures explored. • Challenge and discuss stereotypes (such as inaccurate portrayals of Native Americans) and model acceptance.

Social Studies Standards in Preschool Learning Areas

Blocks

Children can

- participate as a member of the group in a democratic classroom community;
- develop an understanding of location, place, relationships within places, movement, and region.

Building with blocks often involves much negotiation and problem solving for children, providing an opportunity to apply democratic principles of conflict resolution and compromise in action. Children can use blocks to map roads, build buildings, re-create the school or neighborhood, and reflect their growing geographic awareness.

Dramatic Play

Children can

- identify similarities and differences in personal and family characteristics;
- participate as a member of the group in a democratic classroom community;
- increase their understanding about how basic economic concepts relate to their lives;
- appreciate their own and other cultures.

Dramatic play is one of the richest ways in which children demonstrate their growing understanding of the concepts of social studies. In imitating their own families, they are showing their growing sense of self within a family unit and within a broader community. They negotiate with others as role plays develop and learn to compromise and resolve conflicts as citizens do. They portray occupations, show how economics and money issues affect everyday lives, and incorporate different cultural aspects if given the materials and experiences to do so.

Manipulatives

Children can

- increase their understanding about how basic economic concepts relate to their lives;
- develop an understanding of location, place, relationships within places, movement, and region;
- appreciate their own and other cultures.

You can provide puzzles of the United States and a globe of the world for children to explore. Puzzles and games about community helpers and occupations are also common. Adding games and toys from varying cultures expands children's thinking and awareness.

Art

Children can

- identify similarities and differences in personal and family characteristics;
- appreciate their own and other cultures.

As children explore various media, they can represent themselves and their own characteristics in a variety of ways. Providing skin color crayons, paints, and papers helps them accurately look at these personal traits. You can expose children to the many ways different cultures create beautiful items and offer them opportunities to create for themselves.

Social Studies Standards Imbedded in Projects That Follow Upon Children's Interests

The content of social studies is ripe with possibilities for projects and learning since it is centered on the nature of self, family, and community. Children never tire of learning more about themselves, their bodies, their families and traditions, and those of their friends and classmates or of exploring neighborhoods and communities and learning more about adult roles and occupations.

Social Studies Standards That Can Be Imbedded in Large Group Times

Because you and the children are busy establishing a functioning, democratic classroom community, social studies is a part of any group gathering. Problem solving with children about common concerns, exposing them to the similarities and differences among them, and helping them to demonstrate acceptance and kindness are all part of many large group time experiences.

Social Studies Standards That Can Be Imbedded in Small Group Work

You can explore geographic locations with a small group of children, mapping the results or making group murals of places visited. You can trace bodies or body parts, make self-portraits, share personal experiences and family traditions, and explore other cultures. You can read or write stories about adult occupations and act out various adult roles in dramatic play.

Social/Emotional Standards in Action

8

As early educators, you work with children's developing social/emotional capabilities every minute that you are with them. They are learning to separate from family members and develop independence in the greater world. You are ready to earn their trust and help them feel safe and secure in your care. You introduce them to other children and adults and promote a sense of community with kindness, consideration, and friendship at its core. They are learning to express their feelings and often do so through their behavior. You help them learn to do so more through words and spend a lot of time protecting them from harm and modeling conflict resolution with them. You provide a predictable routine yet have the flexibility to recognize when their attention wanders and the resourcefulness to change activities and engage them in ways that sustain their interest. You help them join in groups successfully and develop friendships with other children. You are providing experiences for them that will shape who they will be as human beings and as successful students in later grades.

In this chapter, we have chosen five standards from different states that cover the range of early learning standards in the area of social/emotional development from around the country. We recognize that there are many more ways to address these standards than the ideas we have put forth here. We invite you to think about your classroom and curriculum. How will you address these standards in your program?

Early Learning Standards	Common Practices in an Early Childhood Classroom Where This Standard May Be Addressed
"Standard 1: Children display a healthy self-image in a safe, supportive, and stimulating learning environment. **Benchmark 1.1. The child demonstrates the ability to separate from family and to adjust to new situations."** —*Arizona Early Childhood Education Standards* *Other states with similar standards:* OK	*Helping children transition at arrival time involves assuring them that they can trust you and that their parents will return again. Taking the time for a calm and caring arrival is an important part of beginning the day in a positive way for each child. Some children need help in other transitions throughout the day as well.* Some young children transition between home and school more easily than others. You are ready to step in and comfort a child for whom separation is difficult and to reassure the parent or caregiver as she leaves as well. You offer hugs, a calming voice, and reassuring words at arrival, and consistent nurturing support to the child throughout the day so that he can develop trust and comfort in the school setting and develop the sense of independent and competent self as he separates from his family members and copes with the transitions inherent in a day in an early childhood program.

Access state standards at www.ccsso.org/ECEAstandards. For information correlating state standards, go to www.nieer.org/standards/statelist.php.

	First Steps Toward the Standard:	**Making Progress Toward the Standard:**	**Accomplishing the Standard:**
What the Children Might Show You: A growing sense of comfort in handling transitions	Child cries at arrival or transitions and settles down after comfort from teachers	Child still occasionally cries or expresses concerns at arrival or transitions and is easily comforted	For the most part, child easily manages arrival and transitions throughout the day
Curriculum and Activities that You Can Plan and Implement for Each Child's Progress Level	• As a child arrives, be ready to help her separate by staying with the child, using a calm voice, giving hugs, and easing her into the group activities until settled in. If necessary, call parents to assure them. • As a child works and plays, converse back and forth about the day's schedule, what to expect next, and when a parent will return. • Read books like *The Kissing Hand* and provide strategies to help with separation. • Provide a pictorial schedule of daily activities that is posted for children to see. • Give clear announcements of upcoming activities or any changes in the daily routine. • Be ready to help children at transition times.	• As a child arrives, be ready to help her separate and say "good-bye," staying with the child until she is settled in. • As a child works and plays, converse back and forth and encourage her to tell you about the day's schedule, what to expect next, and when a parent will return. • Ask families for family photos to display on bulletin boards or in a class family photo album. • Have children refer to the pictorial schedule if they are unsure of what comes next. • Have a child help you with announcements of transitions by ringing a bell or setting a timer. • Encourage children to help other children at transition times.	• As a child arrives, greet the child and help her do arrival routines and join in group activities. • As a child works and plays, converse back and forth and encourage her to talk about what to expect next and to help others who are having troubles with transitions. • Have children make their own schedules if they wish or add new items to your class pictorial schedule. • Encourage children to make drawings and paintings to take home. • Document children's days with photographs and observation notes to be displayed or shared in portfolios.

Early Learning Standards	Common Practices in an Early Childhood Classroom Where This Standard May Be Addressed

"SE 2 Children will develop curiosity, initiative, self-direction, and persistence."

—*Georgia Pre-K Program Content Standards*

Other states with similar standards:
MD, NJ, RI

Choosing materials and activities that engage children's interest so that they stay with them for increasing periods of time and persist in solving any problems that arise as they explore. This develops children's attention spans, self-direction, and persistence.

You recognize that the longer a child stays engaged with an activity the more she will discover and learn in the process. One of the primary goals of early education is to help children settle into activities, focus on tasks at hand, and complete them in some way, even though problems may have to be solved to do so. By working to help children sustain attention to tasks, you are building foundational skills that will serve them well as students in the later grades.

Access state standards at www.ccsso.org/ECEAstandards. For information correlating state standards, go to www.nieer.org/standards/statelist.php.

	First Steps Toward the Standard:	**Making Progress Toward the Standard:**	**Accomplishing the Standard:**
What the Children Might Show You: An increasing amount of time spent working and playing with persistence	Stays with a task for up to five minutes; may give up when problem arises	Stays with a task for five to ten minutes and attempts to solve problems that arise	Stays with a task for more than ten minutes and attempts to solve problems that arise

Curriculum and Activities that You Can Plan and Implement for Each Child's Progress Level

- As a child works and plays, comment on what he is doing and give suggestions to extend his play. Be prepared to help when problems arise.

- Provide a variety of materials and experiences for exploration and allow enough time for children to really get involved.

- If a child is flitting from activity to activity, invite him to join you in working with a material that might be of more interest to him. Often sensory items (water, sand, playdough) are more engaging.

- Ask open-ended questions as children explore. This may lead to more interest and challenging use of materials.

- As a child works and plays, comment on what he is doing and encourage him to figure out ways to extend his play and solve problems as they arise.

- Make positive comments about how long children are engaged.

- Describing what children are doing so that the whole group can hear often brings other children to the activity.

- Help children get started with an activity and then slowly let them go on with it themselves. Be ready to provide support or make comments as they work.

- As you ask open-ended questions, encourage children to consider new ways of using and combining materials.

- Continue to engage children in conversations and encourage them to describe what they are doing, extend their play, and solve problems as they arise.

- Continue to help children get started with activities and then take them over for themselves. Be ready to provide support or make comments as they work.

- Encourage children to ask open-ended questions of each other and challenge each other to consider new ways of using and combining materials.

- Follow up by having children review what they did with the large group. Make positive comments about their sustained engagement.

Early Learning Standards

Common Practices in an Early Childhood Classroom Where This Standard May Be Addressed

"Developmental Area: Self-Control

Prior to entering kindergarten, parents and programs will provide learning experiences for children that allow them to:

Express feelings, needs, and opinions appropriately without harming themselves, others, or property"

—*Delaware Early Learning Foundations for School Success*

Other states with similar standards:
CA, CO, CT, DC, GA, IL, IA, LA, MD, MA, MI, MN, MO, NE, NJ, NY, OK, RI, TX, UT

Encouraging children to use words to express their feelings and state their needs and opinions is an ongoing process in early childhood classrooms. Helping children develop impulse control and the ability to refrain from harming anyone or anything is a primary task when working with preschoolers.

You say it again and again with the children: "Use your words. Can you tell him how that makes you feel?" Then you act as mediator between the children involved and encourage each one to become aware of the other's feelings and to resolve their conflict in a kind and considerate way. This is another of those areas that early educators work on extensively with children in order to build the foundation for their capabilities as students in later grades. Young children struggle with controlling strong feelings and need all the help you can give them to assist them in learning self-control within a group setting.

Access state standards at www.ccsso.org/ECEAstandards. For information correlating state standards, go to www.nieer.org/standards/statelist.php.

	First Steps Toward the Standard:	**Making Progress Toward the Standard:**	**Accomplishing the Standard:**
What the Children Might Show You: A growing ability to express feelings, needs, and wants verbally rather than behaviorally	Uses behavior to express feelings but will express verbally after a teacher intervenes and helps	Begins to verbally express feelings on her own but may still need teacher intervention and help to do so	Verbally expresses feelings more often with less need for teacher intervention and help to do so
Curriculum and Activities that You Can Plan and Implement for Each Child's Progress Level	• As a child works and plays, be prepared to step in and model verbal conflict resolution. • Carefully examine the environment where problems seem to arise most frequently. Rearrange furniture, shelving, and number of materials available or number of children working in an area to prevent conflicts. • At group times, talk about ways to work and play together with kindness and consideration. • Read stories and sing songs about feelings and conflict resolution. • Have a safe place for children to go to when they feel out of control or need some time alone. Provide soft pillows for pounding or snuggling.	• As a child works and plays, support verbal expressions of feelings and be prepared to step in and help with conflict resolution. • Think prevention! If you know two children tend to have problems, be nearby or discreetly separate their activities. • Encourage children to ask for help when problems arise. Have signals for getting help from a teacher or a peer. • Recognize and acknowledge acts of kindness and consideration and successful conflict resolution. • Continue to offer a safe place in the classroom. Positively comment when a child makes the choice to go there.	• Continue to support verbal expressions of feelings and be prepared to step in and help with conflict resolution. • Continue to think prevention rather than reaction! • If serious problems are arising during play and work time, stop the action and have a class meeting to discuss and problem-solve together. • At group times, act out feelings or role-play conflict resolution. • Encourage the children to recognize and acknowledge acts of kindness and consideration and successful conflict resolution. • Continue to offer a safe place.

Early Learning Standards	Common Practices in an Early Childhood Classroom Where This Standard May Be Addressed

"Adaptive Social Behavior

Goal: Children participate positively in group activities."

—Washington State Early Learning and Development Benchmarks (Review Draft, 11/04)

Other states with similar standards:

CA, CT, DC, GA, IL, IA, LA, MD, MA, MI, MN, MO, NE, NJ, NY, OK, RI, TX, UT

Providing opportunities every day for children to participate in large and small groups and to feel part of a community of learners in the classroom

You gather the children together throughout the day in order to communicate with them, to read stories and sing songs, to conduct science experiments or play group games, or to transition to snack, outdoors, or departure. Consistently, you work at building a sense of community in these gatherings, joining in consistent rituals, reviewing things you have seen children do, introducing them to upcoming events and experiences, reminding them of rules and procedures, and commenting positively on the ways they are learning and growing every day. You know that group times are only successful as long as you have the interest of the children. So you pay close attention to how attentive they are and try to vary activities and group time length so that you can keep them engaged in constructive discussions and activities. When they lose interest, you transition into the next activity so that group times remain a positive focus for all.

Access state standards at www.ccsso.org/ECEAstandards. For information correlating state standards, go to www.nieer.org/standards/statelist.php.

	First Steps Toward the Standard:	**Making Progress Toward the Standard:**	**Accomplishing the Standard:**
What the Children Might Show You: A growing ability to participate positively in group activities	Comes to group activities for short periods of time; may need adult help (e.g., a lap to sit on)	Comes to group activities for longer periods of time without adult help	Participates actively in group activities for longer periods of time
Curriculum and Activities that You Can Plan and Implement for Each Child's Progress Level	• Build a sense of community among the children by having rituals that gather groups together (songs, chants, special signals, etc.). • Recognize children by name as they join the group. Talk about friends and classmates in positive tones. • Make sure the group gathering area is spacious enough for children to have room to sit without crowding. • Have a staff member be prepared to help any children who are not joining the group, providing a lap to sit on or a gentle back rub. • If a child is disruptive or unable to join in, provide a quiet activity for that child elsewhere with someone able to supervise. • End the group when children's interest fades.	• Build a sense of community among the children by having rituals that gather groups together (songs, chants, special signals, etc.). Let children take turns calling others to group. • Recognize children by name as they join the group. Encourage them to talk about friends and classmates in positive tones. • Begin group times with more physical activity—dancing and moving—and then move to quieter activities (finger plays, discussions, and stories). • Note who is present and absent. Express concern for ill friends. • End the group when children's interest fades. • Have a ritual or procedure for transitioning to the next activity (e.g., finger plays, name cards, etc.).	• Continue to build a sense of community among the children by having rituals that gather groups together. • Play name games and partner movement activities to pull the group together. • Begin group times with more physical activity and then move to quieter activities. Let children choose favorite songs, games, and stories. • Encourage children to note who is present and absent and express concern for ill friends. • End the group when children's interest fades. • Have a ritual or procedure for transitioning to the next activity (e.g., people sorting, chants with names, name cards, etc.).

Early Learning Standards

Common Practices in an Early Childhood Classroom Where This Standard May Be Addressed

"Standard: Children develop the ability to interact with peers respectfully, and to form positive peer relationships.

Benchmarks 2:
The child develops friendships with other peers."

—*Iowa Early Learning Standards*

Other states with similar standards:
CT, IL, MD, MI, NJ, NY, RI, TX, UT

Providing many opportunities for children to play and work together helps them develop friendships and learn more about getting along with other children

You spend much time helping children learn to be friends. You set up an atmosphere of caring and thoughtfulness. You help children learn each other's names and respect each other's feelings. You define what friendship involves and help children express themselves appropriately. You recognize when particular friendships develop among children and encourage the joy that brings to the children involved. And you try to help those children who are not connecting as easily with their peers so that they can enjoy a special friend as well.

Access state standards at www.ccsso.org/ECEAstandards. For information correlating state standards, go to www.nieer.org/standards/statelist.php.

	First Steps Toward the Standard:	Making Progress Toward the Standard:	Accomplishing the Standard:
What the Children Might Show You: A growing interest in special friends	Plays and works alongside other children or watches and imitates others without much concern about anyone special	May play and work with other children without much concern about anyone special	Identifies some children as special friends and chooses to play and work with them often
Curriculum and Activities that You Can Plan and Implement for Each Child's Progress Level	• As a child works and plays, make comments about other children nearby and ways that they could work together. Do not force interaction, but rather comment or model for them. • Encourage children with similar interests to join together in activities. • At group times, talk about ways to work and play together with kindness and consideration. • Read stories and sing songs about friends and friendships. • Pair a shyer child with a more outgoing one in some activities. • Be a special friend yourself to a child who is often alone. Invite others to join the two of you at work and play.	• As a child works and plays, make comments about ways that children are working together. • Recognize and acknowledge acts of kindness, consideration, and friendship. • Read stories and sing songs about friends and friendships. • Encourage children to invite and include other children in their play and work. • Help a shyer child play alongside or join a more outgoing group in some activities. Be prepared to stay until the child is successfully included. • Intervene when children are excluded, talking through the feelings involved and helping the group be more inclusive.	• Continue to support children's friendships and interactions with each other. • Make class books about all of the children with photos, interests, likes, and dislikes. Read frequently to get to know each other better. • At group times, act out ways to be friends or to make new friends. • Encourage the children to recognize and acknowledge acts of kindness, consideration, and friendship. • Continue to help shyer children find entries into play. • Continue to intervene when children are excluded.

Social/Emotional Standards in Preschool Learning Areas

Blocks

Children can

- develop curiosity, initiative, self-direction, and persistence;
- express feelings, needs, and opinions appropriately without harming themselves, others, or property;
- participate positively in group activities.

Building with blocks often involves sticking with a task as structures fall and topple. In addition, much negotiation with others might be involved in group construction play.

Dramatic Play

Children can

- demonstrate the ability to separate from family and to adjust to new situations;
- express feelings, needs, and opinions appropriately without harming themselves, others, or property;
- participate positively in group activities;
- develop friendships with peers.

Through role playing, children explore expression of feelings, development of relationships, and conflict resolution. As they imitate their own family members, they may be dealing with their own feelings of separation from loved ones.

Class Library and Writing Center

Children can

- develop curiosity, initiative, self-direction, and persistence;
- express feelings, needs, and opinions appropriately without harming themselves, others, or property;
- develop friendships with peers.

Many stories about feelings and friendships are available to help children explore ways to express themselves appropriately and develop caring relationships with others. Children can write letters to friends and family and make class books about friendship and feelings.

Arrival Time

Children can

- demonstrate the ability to separate from family and to adjust to new situations;
- express feelings, needs, and opinions appropriately without harming themselves, others, or property;
- develop friendships with peers.

Arrival time can be difficult for some children. Providing calm, reassuring rituals for saying good-bye and offering ways to express feelings of sadness through drawing or other creative activity can help the transition. New friends can offer their company and support as well.

Social/Emotional Standards Imbedded in Projects That Follow Upon Children's Interests

Children's interest in themselves extends to their feelings for their friends as well. Learning can focus on taking surveys of others in the group to learn their interests and experiences.

Social/Emotional Standards That Can Be Imbedded in Large Group Times

Large group times are times to build a community of caring friends, to problem-solve conflicts that have arisen, and to enjoy some fun activities together as well.

Social/Emotional Standards That Can Be Imbedded in Small Group Work

Working in small groups allows more intimacy and discussion about feelings, friendships, and conflicts. Making books and drawings together, learning to work cooperatively toward a common goal, and having close interaction with a caring adult can all happen more easily in a small group setting.

Physical Development and Health Standards in Action

9

Young children's bodies are growing and need physical activity and nutritional foods to thrive and develop. Providing gross motor activities with safe supervision by caring adults will help young muscles develop coordination and strength. Being available to provide support for a fearful child

during active play is important to develop his confidence in his motor skills. In addition, giving children opportunities to try out various tools and materials that will help their hand-eye coordination and fine motor skills is important. In order to write and draw, to type on computer keyboards, and to manipulate objects in life, children's hand muscles must be stimulated and challenged. Again, providing just the right materials so that children experience success as they learn basic skills, e.g., cutting with scissors, writing and drawing with markers, and putting together puzzles and pegboards, is important. We build skills in the beginning by creating opportunities for success so that challenges do not feel so frightening or out of reach for

children as they are developing. Finally, teaching children about healthful diets, nutritional foods, and the importance of exercise are all part of our responsibilities as educators in the area of physical development and health.

In this chapter, we have chosen five standards from different states that cover the range of early learning standards in the area of physical development and health from around the country. We recognize that there are many more ways to address these standards than the ideas we have put forth here. We invite you to think about your classroom and curriculum. How will you address these standards in your program?

Early Learning Standards	Common Practices in an Early Childhood Classroom Where This Standard May Be Addressed

"Pre K–Kindergarten Standard 3: Select and participate in physical activity during unscheduled times."

—*South Carolina Physical Education Curriculum Standards*

Other states with similar standards:
CT, GA, IL, LA, MD, MI, MN, NJ, NY, RI, TX

Providing opportunities for physical activity both indoors and out, encouraging children to expend energy and use their bodies to their fullest capabilities

You schedule times for children to play outdoors on safe equipment with opportunities and room to run, jump, climb, swing, ride tricycles, play with balls, and use their large muscles to the fullest. You know that expending energy is important and that physical activity is healthy for children's hearts, lungs, and minds. You also provide opportunities indoors for children to be active through movement games, dancing, and hands-on activities with materials in the classroom. You try to balance quiet, more passive times with active, moving times so that children can channel their energies more positively.

Access state standards at www.ccsso.org/ECEAstandards. For information correlating state standards, go to www.nieer.org/standards/statelist.php.

	First Steps Toward the Standard:	Making Progress Toward the Standard:	Accomplishing the Standard:
What the Children Might Show You: Participation in a range of physical activities indoors and out	Participates in some physical activities indoors and out (may sometimes watch instead)	Participates in more physical activities indoors and out (rarely chooses not to do so)	Participates in many physical activities indoors and out (rarely chooses not to do so)
Curriculum and Activities that You Can Plan and Implement for Each Child's Progress Level	• Provide at least one extended outdoor time (twenty to thirty minutes) on safe equipment with adult supervision throughout the outdoor area. • Offer additional materials to use outdoors periodically such as balls, ropes, bubbles, water play, and sand toys. • Occasionally, organize outdoor group games for those interested (e.g., relay races, Duck Duck Goose, etc.). • Offer physical activities indoors: play movement games, dance to music using scarves, hop and tiptoe on the ABC rug, be a marching band with rhythm instruments. • Encourage children to try out different activities. Help a reticent child find something of interest and respect if she refuses.	• Provide at least one extended outdoor time (twenty to thirty minutes) on safe equipment with adult supervision throughout the outdoor area. • Invite children to suggest additional materials to use outdoors periodically (e.g., paint easels, bowling game, wind streamers, etc.). • Help the children organize outdoor group games for those interested and provide support and supervision. • Offer physical activities indoors and invite children to initiate their favorites. • Encourage children to try out different activities. Help a reticent child find something of interest and respect if she refuses.	• Provide at least one extended outdoor time (twenty to thirty minutes) on safe equipment with adult supervision throughout the outdoor area. • Invite children to suggest additional materials to use outdoors periodically. Have a picnic snack. Set up a driver's license test for bike riders. Follow an obstacle course. • Encourage children to organize outdoor group games for those interested. • Invite children to initiate their favorite indoor physical activities. • Encourage children to try out different activities and to help a more reticent child find something of interest. Still do respect if she refuses.

Early Learning Standards

Common Practices in an Early Childhood Classroom Where This Standard May Be Addressed

"VII. Physical Health and Development Domain/Content Area

(A) Gross Motor Skills Standard:

The child demonstrates control, balance, strength and coordination in gross motor tasks."

—*Wyoming Early Childhood Readiness Standards*

Other states with similar standards:
CA, CT, IL, IA, LA, MD, MA, MI, MN, NE, NJ, NY, OK, RI, TX, UT

Throughout the physical activities that you are providing both indoors and out for the children, you are observing their gross motor skills and general coordination and offering support and challenges according to their motor capabilities

Some children have more coordination and comfort with their bodies than others. Recognizing that each child develops his gross motor skills in his own time and that each will have his own strengths and weaknesses in the physical area, you provide a range of activities and adult support so that children can develop the confidence and muscular control to enjoy success at a variety of tasks.

Access state standards at www.ccsso.org/ECEAstandards. For information correlating state standards, go to www.nieer.org/standards/statelist.php.

	First Steps Toward the Standard:	**Making Progress Toward the Standard:**	**Accomplishing the Standard:**
What the Children Might Show You: Increasing bodily control, balance, strength, and coordination	Shows comfort and capabilities with some gross motor tasks and avoids others (e.g., runs and jumps but does not climb on equipment)	Shows comfort and capabilities with more gross motor tasks and will try others with adult support and encouragement	Shows comfort and capabilities with many gross motor tasks and will try others with adult support and encouragement
Curriculum and Activities that You Can Plan and Implement for Each Child's Progress Level	• Provide a variety of physical activities outdoors that require control, balance, strength, and coordination (climbers, swings, balance beams, hanging bars, running paths, tricycles, balls, etc.). • Provide a variety of physical activities indoors (obstacle courses, small trampoline, movement games, dancing, relay races, balloons and streamers, etc.). • Notice the children who show fear or avoidance of certain equipment or activities. Do not force them to participate. Be encouraging and reassuring. • Take observation notes of children's gross motor capabilities.	• Provide a variety of physical activities indoors and out that require control, balance, strength, and coordination. • Offer assistance and support to children who show fear or avoidance of certain equipment or activities. Let them tell you what they are willing to try. • Take observation notes of children's gross motor capabilities. • Recognize children's new skills and attempts at trying out new activities or equipment. Celebrate their risk taking and accomplishments with them. • Discuss the health aspects of exercise and activity with them.	• Provide a variety of physical activities indoors and out that require control, balance, strength, and coordination. • Be ready to assist children who show fear or avoidance of certain equipment or activities. • Recognize and celebrate their new skills and risk taking. • Take observation notes and photographs of children's gross motor capabilities. Invite children to share their accomplishments with you so you can document them. • Read books about healthy bodies and exercise. • Make stretching and balancing moves part of group times.

Early Learning Standards	Common Practices in an Early Childhood Classroom Where This Standard May Be Addressed

"Learning Goals and Definitions:

3. Fine Motor

Children use their fingers and hands in ways that develop hand-eye coordination, strength, control and object manipulation."

—*Rhode Island Early Learning Standards*

Other states with similar standards:
CA, CT, GA, IA, LA, MD, MA, MI, MN, MO, NE, NJ, OK, TX, UT

Offering a variety of materials and activities that require fine motor coordination, including playdough and clay, small building blocks and connecting toys, puzzles of varying pieces and sizes, pegs and pegboards, geo-boards, lacing cards, stringing beads, scissors, hole punchers, and tweezers

You have your classroom environment organized into learning areas that contain tools and materials that will help children develop a variety of skills. Specific areas require more fine motor coordination: the art area, the manipulatives area, the writing center. In these areas, you provide a variety of tools and materials so that children can try out their abilities to use their fingers and hands and increase their hand-eye coordination.

Access state standards at www.ccsso.org/ECEAstandards. For information correlating state standards, go to www.nieer.org/standards/statelist.php.

	First Steps Toward the Standard:	Making Progress Toward the Standard:	Accomplishing the Standard:
What the Children Might Show You: Increasing hand-eye coordination, strength, control, and object manipulation	Shows comfort and capabilities with some fine motor tasks and avoids others (e.g., draws with markers but does not use scissors)	Shows comfort and capabilities with more fine motor tasks and will try others with adult support and encouragement	Shows comfort and capabilities with many fine motor tasks and will try others with adult support and encouragement
Curriculum and Activities that You Can Plan and Implement for Each Child's Progress Level	• Provide a variety of fine motor materials and activities and specific classroom areas where they can be explored. • Notice the children who show avoidance of certain materials or activities. Do not force them to participate. • Provide an array of sizes of similar objects so that children can experience success (e.g., Duplo and Lego building blocks, simple knob puzzles moving up to puzzles with many pieces, large and small pegs and pegboards, large and small stringing beads). • Take observation notes of children's fine motor capabilities.	• Provide a variety of fine motor materials, tools, and activities and specific classroom areas where they can be explored. • Offer assistance and support to children who show avoidance of certain materials or activities. Let them tell you what they are willing to try. Give them larger items to start with to build their success and confidence. • Take observation notes and photos of children's creations with manipulatives for their portfolios. • Recognize children's new skills and attempts at trying out new activities or materials. Celebrate their accomplishments!	• Provide a variety of fine motor materials, tools, and activities and specific classroom areas where they can be explored. • Be ready to assist children who show fear or avoidance of certain materials or activities. • Recognize and celebrate children's new skills. • Take observation notes and photos to document fine motor capabilities. Invite children to share their accomplishments with you. • Display photos of children's work with manipulatives throughout the classroom.

Early Learning Standards

Common Practices in an Early Childhood Classroom Where This Standard May Be Addressed

"Standard IV: Children will use their bodies optimally to explore, negotiate and manipulate the environment.

Benchmark C: Child demonstrates increasing skill with tabletop activities.

Indicator: Manipulates writing and/or painting utensils (e.g., sponge, paintbrush, pencil)."

—*New Mexico Performance Standards and Benchmarks for Three and Four Year Olds*

Other states with similar standards:
CA, CT, GA, LA, MD, MA, MI, MN, MO, NJ, OK, RI, TX, UT

Providing tools and utensils for self-expression through painting, drawing, and writing not only gives children the opportunity to explore their creativity and early literacy skills, but helps them develop the control and coordination needed to use these tools effectively

You equip your writing and art areas with a variety of utensils to help children learn to use these tools to paint, create, draw, and write. You know that the more varied the selection, the more successes children will have. Some children need thick brushes and markers in order to get the results they want and to feel successful in doing so. Other children will challenge their fine motor control by choosing thinner crayons and pencils for their creations. You are ready to help them find the tools that work best for them and learn to grasp them appropriately so that they can represent their thoughts and ideas in the best ways for them.

	First Steps Toward the Standard:	Making Progress Toward the Standard:	Accomplishing the Standard:
What the Children Might Show You: A growing ability to successfully use tools and utensils for self-expression	Uses tools and utensils with some control and success, grasping them with fist or fingertips inappropriately	Uses tools and utensils with more control and success, using an appropriate grasp most of the time	Uses tools and utensils with more control and success, consistently using an appropriate grasp
Curriculum and Activities that You Can Plan and Implement for Each Child's Progress Level	• Provide a variety of fine motor tools in the writing and art areas. • Notice the children who show avoidance of certain materials or activities. Do not force them to participate. • A child who chooses not to use writing and drawing tools may prefer working with play-dough or painting with large brushes (requiring less fine motor coordination). Offer these opportunities as alternatives to writing and drawing. • Encourage children to try drawing and writing with thicker markers rather than pencils or crayons so they have more success. • Take observation notes of children's fine motor capabilities.	• Provide a variety of fine motor tools in the writing and art areas. • Offer assistance and support to children who show avoidance of certain materials or activities. Let them tell you what they are willing to try. • Include writing and drawing tools in a variety of other areas of the classroom (e.g., for making signs in the block area, for taking phone messages in the house corner). • Take observation notes and invite children to share work samples (drawings, writing, and cutting) with you. • Recognize children's new skills and attempts at trying out new activities or materials. Celebrate!	• Provide a variety of fine motor tools in the writing and art areas. • Be ready to assist children who show avoidance of certain materials or activities. • Recognize and celebrate children's new skills. • Take observation notes, collect work samples, and take photographs to document fine motor capabilities. Invite children to share their accomplishments with you. • Set up purposes for writing: daily sign-in, sign-in sheets at learning areas, a class post office, a message board. • Display children's art work and writing samples throughout the classroom.

Early Learning Standards	Common Practices in an Early Childhood Classroom Where This Standard May Be Addressed

"Standard 6.0: Students will demonstrate the ability to use nutrition and fitness knowledge, skills, and strategies to promote a healthy lifestyle.

Indicators: A. Nutrition and Fitness

8. Tell the relationship between food and health."

—*Maryland Model for School Readiness Frameworks and Standards for PreKindergarten (Draft 2004)*

Other states with similar standards:
CA, CT, GA, LA, MD, NJ, RI, TX

Introducing concepts of nutrition through healthful snacks, cooking activities, and meals as well as through books and group discussions

You provide a consistent snack time and may provide meals as well for the children in your care. To meet best practices, licensing standards, and state health requirements, you make sure that the foods you serve are nutritious. And you discuss eating habits, different types of foods, and ways to eat for health with the children as you prepare and eat foods together.

	First Steps Toward the Standard:	Making Progress Toward the Standard:	Accomplishing the Standard:
What the Children Might Show You: A growing awareness of and vocabulary to identify nutritious foods	Begins to show some awareness of the relationship between health and nutritious food	Shows some accuracy when comparing healthful and non-healthful foods	Shows more accuracy when comparing healthful and non-healthful foods
Curriculum and Activities that You Can Plan and Implement for Each Child's Progress Level	• Prepare and serve nutritious snacks and meals daily. • Sit with the children at snacks and mealtimes and discuss the foods served. Point out ways that they provide nutrition to help them grow. • Discuss children's favorite foods and introduce vocabulary words, "healthy," "nutritious," "junk food," etc. • Prepare foods with children, discussing ingredients and health benefits. • Include information about nutrition in parent newsletters and announcements.	• Prepare and serve nutritious snacks and meals daily. • In snack and mealtime conversations with children, encourage them to identify how the foods being served help them to grow. • Make graphs of favorite foods and categorize as healthful and not healthful. • Play food classification games categorizing food into fruits, vegetables, etc., and identifying healthful versus not healthful. • Prepare healthful foods with children, discussing ingredients and health benefits. Have children write or draw the recipe and preparation steps to share at home.	• Prepare and serve nutritious snacks and meals daily and converse with children about health benefits, favorite foods, categories of foods, and good eating habits. • Invite children to help plan menus. Evaluate for health benefits and nutritional value. • Make class books about favorite foods or about favorite categories like fruits or vegetables. • Read books about health and nutrition. • Invite families to share favorite healthful recipes that may reflect cultural backgrounds. • Produce a class cookbook.

Physical Development and Health Standards in Preschool Learning Areas

Blocks

Children can

- demonstrate control, balance, strength, and coordination in gross motor tasks;
- use their fingers and hands in ways that develop hand-eye coordination, strength, control, and object manipulation.

Building with large blocks involves large muscles, while building with smaller ones requires fine motor coordination.

Dramatic Play

Children can

- demonstrate control, balance, strength, and coordination in gross motor tasks;
- use their fingers and hands in ways that develop hand-eye coordination, strength, control, and object manipulation.

As children act out characters in play, they use their bodies in different ways (crawling like a baby or a kitty, standing tall like a dad, fighting off the bad guys in superhero play). They also use their fine motor skills to put on dress-up clothes and shoes.

Manipulatives

Children can

- use their fingers and hands in ways that develop hand-eye coordination, strength, control, and object manipulation.

Puzzles, pegboards, stringing beads, connecting blocks, play-dough, and clay all help develop hand muscles.

Art Area and Writing Area

Children can

- use their fingers and hands in ways that develop hand-eye coordination, strength, control, and object manipulation;
- manipulate writing and/or painting utensils (e.g., sponge, paintbrush, pencil).

As children express themselves through drawing, painting, and writing, they develop control of tools and utensils.

Outdoor and Indoor Physical Activities

Children can

- select and participate in physical activity during unscheduled times;
- demonstrate control, balance, strength, and coordination in gross motor tasks.

Offering a wide selection of physical activities both indoors and out helps children move their bodies and explore their own physical capabilities.

Cooking, Snacks, and Mealtimes

Children can

- use their fingers and hands in ways that develop hand-eye coordination, strength, control, and object manipulation;
- tell the relationship between food and health.

You can help children learn more about nutrition and health by involving them in preparing and eating a variety of healthful foods. They also use fine motor skills in stirring, measuring, setting tables, using eating utensils, and pouring with pitchers.

Physical Development and Health Standards Imbedded in Projects That Follow Upon Children's Interests

Including gross motor exploration in a study or project keeps children interested and helps them use their energies to the fullest. In a study of balls, it's important to try throwing, kicking, and rolling balls to see what happens. In a study of trees or birds, taking walks and observing outdoors will be the way to gather information. Fine motor skills come into play as children document what they are learning through drawings and writing.

Physical Development and Health Standards That Can Be Imbedded in Large Group Times

As children join in movement games and dancing activities, they use their gross motor skills. Finger plays involve the fine motor skills.

Physical Development and Health Standards That Can Be Imbedded in Small Group Work

Small groups can be the time to check in on children's physical capabilities and take some observation notes regarding their ability to hop or skip, to cut, and to use a writing tool.

Creative Arts Standards in Action

10

Young children express themselves creatively in many ways. They act out a range of familiar and imagined scenes in dramatic play, increasing in complexity and involvement as they go. They enjoy the process of working with materials such as paints, the makings for collage, markers and paper, or clay and playdough and do not worry about accurate representation or "looking nice or right." You provide them with a variety of materials and plenty of time to explore various media. You accept their creations, displaying them and helping parents understand the importance of the process rather than the final product. Young children also enjoy learning more about other artists. Exposing them to different techniques and styles of visual art may stimulate them to try something different and begin to be conscious of aesthetic differences in expression. Music and movement are other ways young children express themselves creatively. Rhythm, musical dynamics, and melody all add to the classroom atmosphere as you sing with children, make up chants to help with transitions throughout the day, and provide movement and dancing activities to a variety of styles of music. Creative arts truly enrich the early childhood classroom and curriculum and help to develop the whole person as children prepare for school and life. (You will not see any correlations to other states' standards on the charts as the NIEER Web site does not address creative arts in its correlations at this time.)

In this chapter, we have chosen five standards from different states that cover the range of early learning standards in the area of creative arts from around the country. We recognize that there are many more ways to address these standards than the ideas we have put forth here. We invite you to think about your classroom and curriculum. How will you address these standards in your program?

Early Learning Standards	Common Practices in an Early Childhood Classroom Where This Standard May Be Addressed

"Content Standard: Creative Expression/ Aesthetic Development:

Preschool programs will provide children with opportunities to: represent fantasy and real-life experiences through pretend play. . . ."

"Performance Standards (Indicators): Educational experiences will assure that preschool children will: . . . assume the role of someone or something else and talk in the language/tone appropriate for that person or thing."

—*Connecticut's Preschool Curriculum Framework*

Setting up a dramatic play area equipped with dress-up clothes to imitate a number of adult roles and occupations; household items such as a play stove, refrigerator, sink, cabinets, tables, and chairs along with dishes, pots and pans, silverware, and play food items; and baby dolls and clothing representing a variety of ethnicities and cultures

You know that young children are imaginative and can act out elaborate scripts of their own creation. You also recognize how they weave knowledge they are gaining about family life, about interpersonal relationships, and about adult roles and occupations into their pretend play in a way to make sense of their world. As they work with other children in the dramatic play area, they are developing language and social skills and learning to work with abstract thoughts—all of which will prepare them to be better readers, writers, and mathematicians as they move on to the later grades.

Access state standards at www.ccsso.org/ECEAstandards. For information correlating state standards, go to www.nieer.org/standards/statelist.php.

	First Steps Toward the Standard:	**Making Progress Toward the Standard:**	**Accomplishing the Standard:**
What the Children Might Show You: A growing complexity in dramatic play activities	Plays out simple imitations of familiar characters (e.g., Mom, Dad, teacher, dog); may involve one or two other children	Plays out more involved scripts of familiar characters (e.g., Mom, Dad, teacher, dog); may involve more children	Plays out more involved and lengthy scripts with a variety of characters involving several children
Curriculum and Activities that You Can Plan and Implement for Each Child's Progress Level	• Provide a dramatic play area equipped with household items, dress-up clothes, and ethnically varied baby dolls. • Help children get started playing in this area. Ask them to cook for you or help them put on dress-up clothes. Model ways to pretend to eat or drink. • Narrate children's play, providing a running commentary. Ask open-ended questions of the players ("What will happen next?"). • Always be ready to step out as children take the play and make it their own.	• Provide a dramatic play area equipped with household items, dress-up clothes, and ethnically varied baby dolls. • Invite other children to join in and help them extend the play beyond simple imitation, suggesting different characters or aspects of family life to portray. • Document children's play through observation notes and photographs for their portfolios. Share the stories of their scripts with the group at circle time ("Once upon a time, Jessica and Mariselle were playing mommies. . . ."). This will encourage children's play. • Offer other items to change the nature of the role playing: doctor's bag and stethoscope, cash register.	• Provide a dramatic play area equipped with household items, dress-up clothes, and ethnically varied baby dolls. • Pay close attention to the characters and scripts children are acting out. Offer materials to support hospital, store, or restaurant play. • Encourage children to figure out items that can stand in for other items (a block can be a cell phone; paper strips can be play money). • Help children to include others and negotiate any conflicts as the play progresses. • Encourage children to tell you about their play. Add their comments to your observation notes and photos for portfolios.

Early Learning Standards	Common Practices in an Early Childhood Classroom Where This Standard May Be Addressed

"Visual Arts—Pre-Kindergarten

Media, Techniques and Processes

Content Standard 1: Each student will understand and apply media, techniques, and process in the creation and production of art."

—*District of Columbia Public Schools Standards for Teaching and Learning*

Setting up an art area with a variety of materials for children to try out different media and techniques for expressing themselves creatively, including: tempura and watercolor paints with varying size paintbrushes; various sizes and colors of paper for painting, cutting, and drawing; playdough and clay; glue or paste; and a variety of collage materials such as scissors, hole punchers, yarn, string, beads, glitter, crayons, markers, etc.

You have seen young children's creativity in action and know that it is a way that they express feelings and ideas and explore the properties and processes involved in using different artistic materials. You know that the resulting product is not important—rather, the child's experience in the process is the focus.

	First Steps Toward the Standard:	Making Progress Toward the Standard:	Accomplishing the Standard:
What the Children Might Show You: An increasing willingness to express creativity using different materials and techniques	Uses a few materials and techniques as they are introduced by the teachers without combining or trying out in different ways	Uses more materials and techniques and may combine them or try different ways of using them	Uses many materials and techniques and combines them or tries different ways of using them
Curriculum and Activities that You Can Plan and Implement for Each Child's Progress Level	• Provide an art area equipped with a variety of materials. • Introduce children to the different media and techniques, slowly offering new opportunities and materials as they show interest. • Respond to children's creations by describing what they have done, making open-ended, non-evaluative comments (e.g., "You used lots of colors in your painting!"). • Ask if you may display some of their creations for others to see. Share with parents as well as other children, labeling comments the child made about her thinking and process of creation.	• Provide an art area equipped with a variety of materials. Periodically, add new materials and introduce them to the children. • Encourage children to talk about their creations by describing what they have done. • Include their comments on the art work or in your observation notes for their portfolios. Ask if you may save their work or take a photograph of it for the portfolio. • Encourage children to try combining materials or make positive comments as they try a new way to use a material or process. • Include art books in your class library and point out techniques.	• Provide an art area equipped with a variety of materials. Periodically, add new materials and introduce them to the children. • Create a class art gallery and have periodic "openings" when artists can tell more about their work to the class. • Include their comments and art work in their portfolios. • Challenge children to try combining materials or make positive comments as they try a new material or process. • Include art books in your class library and try out different techniques (e.g., Eric Carle's watercolors, pointillism, painting upside down like Michelangelo).

Early Learning Standards	Common Practices in an Early Childhood Classroom Where This Standard May Be Addressed

"Creative Arts Guideline 1: Art Appreciation
You may see the child begin to: express feelings about art."

—*Montana's Early Learning Guidelines*

Exposing children to different types of art through books, posters and illustrations, visits from artists and artisans from a variety of cultures, and field trips to art museums and artists' studios

You enrich children's own creativity by exposing them to the creativity of others. You express acceptance toward children's explorations of media and invite them to express their own reactions and consider how other artists go about expressing themselves as they illustrate books, paint canvases, make drawings, and design sculptures and buildings. Picasso said he spent his life trying to learn how to paint like a child. Early educators can value the freedom from constraints that young children feel as they explore different media and learn to appreciate the works of others.

Access state standards at www.ccsso.org/ECEAstandards. For information correlating state standards, go to www.nieer.org/standards/statelist.php.

	First Steps Toward the Standard:	Making Progress Toward the Standard:	Accomplishing the Standard:
What the Children Might Show You: The inclusion of increasing details when responding to others' creations	Only states a like or dislike	States a like or dislike and identifies some characteristics of the work that he finds interesting	States a like or dislike and supports his opinions describing specific characteristics of the work
Curriculum and Activities that You Can Plan and Implement for Each Child's Progress Level	• Provide an art area equipped with a variety of materials. Introduce children to the different media and techniques. • Show how other artists have used these techniques in book illustrations, posters, and books with paintings and photos of sculptures and buildings. • Respond to children's creations by describing what they have done, making open-ended, non-evaluative comments (e.g., "You used lots of colors in your painting!"). • Encourage children to talk about their likes and dislikes as they look at art books or consider their own creations.	• Provide an art area equipped with a variety of materials. Periodically, add new materials and introduce them to the children. • Encourage children to talk about their creations by describing what they have done. • Share art books with children, study famous children's book illustrators, invite artists and artisans to visit the class and share their techniques and work. • Encourage children to talk about their likes and dislikes as they are exposed to more works of art. Try to elicit descriptive words to support their preferences. • Make a class art gallery that includes prints of famous paintings.	• Provide an art area equipped with a variety of materials. Periodically, add new materials and introduce them to the children. • Encourage children to talk about their own and others' artwork. Encourage use of descriptive words to support their preferences. • Go on field trips to art museums, sculpture gardens, artists' studios, cultural art displays. Follow up with group discussions. • Invite an artisan to share a cultural specialty (e.g., Russian painted eggs). Follow up with creating that specialty in class. • Add architecture books to the block area. Note different styles.

Early Learning Standards

Common Practices in an Early Childhood Classroom Where This Standard May Be Addressed

"The Arts

Standard 1: Music and Movement

Learning Criteria: Each child will participate in a variety of music and movement activities."

—*West Virginia Early Learning Standards Framework*

Singing, dancing, chanting, using instruments, playing movement games, and listening to music of all types helps children explore another way to express themselves

You know that children respond to rhythm, sing just for the sheer joy of it, express feelings through exuberant movements, and are calmed or excited by a variety of musical styles. You use music and chants to help children take care of daily routines like cleanup or transition to other activities. You teach them your favorite songs and finger plays and repeat them as a form of ritual in building community in the classroom. You pull out favorite dance records and movement games so that children can expend energy and develop more gross motor skills. And you give children opportunities to create their own music with rhythm instruments, to learn about beat and keeping time, and to play loudly and softly.

Access state standards at www.ccsso.org/ECEAstandards. For information correlating state standards, go to www.nieer.org/standards/statelist.php.

	First Steps Toward the Standard:	Making Progress Toward the Standard:	Accomplishing the Standard:
What the Children Might Show You: Participation in a range of music and movement activities	Participates in some music and movement activities (may sometimes watch instead)	Participates in music and movement activities (rarely chooses not to do so)	Participates in many music and movement activities (rarely chooses not to do so)
Curriculum and Activities that You Can Plan and Implement for Each Child's Progress Level	• Include music and movement throughout the day, using songs and chants to help move the daily routine along and involve children in transitions. • Whether children join in with you or not, show enthusiasm as you sing and chant throughout the day and invite them to join you. • Include songs, finger plays, or recorded movement games or dances as part of most large group times. Encourage children to join in and respect their right to watch. • Periodically, bring out rhythm instruments and invite children to be a marching band or an orchestra. Conduct them to play loudly, softly, fast, slow. • Play recordings of different types of music throughout the day or have a listening center available.	• Include music and movement throughout the day, using songs and chants to help move the daily routine along and involve children in transitions. • Show enthusiasm as you sing and chant throughout the day and recognize children as they join in. • Have a song leader who chooses familiar songs, finger plays, or recordings for large group times. • Act out familiar songs and finger plays (Five Little Monkeys, Ten in the Bed, Going to the Zoo). • Play different types of music and discuss how it makes you feel. • Encourage children to dance or move to different musical styles. Have clear signals for settling down.	• Encourage children to lead or make up songs and chants to help move the daily routine along. • Have a song leader who chooses familiar songs, finger plays, or recordings for large group times. • Make a class songbook with the words to familiar songs and finger plays in it. Let the song leader point along with the words. • Change the words to familiar songs and finger plays using names of the children or situations that happened at school. • Play movement game recordings from Hap Palmer (Shake Something) or Greg and Steve (Ball and Jack), etc.

Early Learning Standards	Common Practices in an Early Childhood Classroom Where This Standard May Be Addressed

"Creative Arts: Movement

Widely Held Expectations:

Child responds to music through movement. Responds to the beat of songs or instrumental music with more complex movements (walking or jumping to the beat)."

—*Nebraska Early Learning Guidelines for Ages 3 to 5*

Offering a variety of movement activities that include songs or instrumental music encourages children to explore different ways to express themselves with their bodies and to respond to the stimulation of the beat, tempo, and dynamics of the music

In addition to providing movement activities to help children expend energy and transition to activities throughout the day, you plan movement activities that help them learn more about music and dance. You encourage them to march to or clap along with the beat of a song. You play instrumental music recordings and invite them to move in ways that the tempo suggests. You point out dynamics as music gets louder or softer and help them respond in their movement and expression appropriately. You provide scarves or streamers for them to sway along with the music. You are helping them pay attention to the feeling and mood of different musical styles and respond through dance and physical expression.

	First Steps Toward the Standard:	Making Progress Toward the Standard:	Accomplishing the Standard:
What the Children Might Show You: A growing responsiveness through movement to musical styles	Moves to music in ways that may not be related to the style (e.g., runs wildly to soft, slow music) (may sometimes watch instead)	Moves to music in ways that have at least one relation to the style (e.g., following the beat or responding to the volume changes) (rarely choosing to watch instead)	Moves to music in ways that have more than one relation to the style (rarely choosing to watch instead)
Curriculum and Activities that You Can Plan and Implement for Each Child's Progress Level	• Plan for movement to a variety of musical styles as a part of large and small group times on a regular basis. • Set up the movement activity by explaining good listening to the children. As musical styles change, encourage them to "freeze" and listen before they begin to move. • Encourage children to participate and accept those who would rather watch at first. Provide a safe seating place for them. • Follow up any movement to music with quiet discussion. Ask questions such as "How did that music make you feel?" "Was it fast? Slow? Loud? Soft?" • Model different movements.	• Plan for movement to music as a part of large and small group times on a regular basis. • Play freeze games to help children listen to the music and identify the style or musical characteristics. Point out the beat and clap or move along with it. • Have a movement leader who chooses familiar songs, movement games, or recordings for the group. • Add scarves and crepe paper streamers to the dance experience. Classical waltz music is great with these materials. • Play different types of music and discuss how it makes you feel, and then decide how you would move to show that feeling.	• Plan for movement to music as a part of large and small group times on a regular basis. • Have a movement leader who chooses familiar songs, movement games, or recordings for the group. • Add the group's favorite musical recordings to your listening center. Or have a special dance area during activity time. • Show videos of different types of dancing: ballet, modern, flamenco, square dancing, and dances from different cultures. Discuss and imitate in dance experiences. • Visit a dance concert or studio.

Creative Arts Standards in Preschool Learning Areas

Blocks and Dramatic Play

Children can

- assume the role of someone or something else and talk in the language/tone appropriate for that person or thing.

Children often combine dramatic play with their construction with blocks. They use the blocks to represent items in the abstract and enhance the complexity of the scripts they are developing about family life or other familiar parts of their world.

Art Area

Children can

- understand and apply media, techniques, and processes in the creation and production of art;
- express feelings about art.

Providing a variety of materials and introducing different creative techniques gives children many opportunities to express themselves creatively and explore different media. Adding art books and posters to the art area and pointing out different techniques of artists stimulates their aesthetic appreciation and may capture their interest in imitating those techniques.

Music Area

Children can

- participate in a variety of music and movement activities;
- respond to the beat of songs or instrumental music with more complex movements (walking or jumping to the beat, clapping, etc.).

Providing a listening center or playing musical recordings throughout the day helps children incorporate music in their lives and sets a mood in the classroom. Setting up movement activities that require responsiveness to the music helps children learn to use their bodies in different ways and express themselves through dance. Singing favorite songs and chanting familiar finger plays builds community among the group and helps with transitions between activities.

Creative Arts Standards Imbedded in Projects That Follow Upon Children's Interests

Most projects and studies require children to document what they are learning. Drawings, paintings, constructions, and photo representations can all be created to show others the information and concepts that are being explored.

Creative Arts Standards That Can Be Imbedded in Large Group Times

Every large group time should include movement to music, as well as singing and chanting of favorite songs and finger plays. Planning group times to move from more physical and active involvement to quieter sitting and listening helps children be successful in settling down with many other children. Large group time can also be used to look at art books and introduce new media for the art area, to recognize children's creations in the classroom, to revisit their dramatic play scripts, and to encourage them to try new ways of exploring their creativity in all the areas of the classroom.

Creative Arts Standards That Can Be Imbedded in Small Group Work

Some creative projects can be done as a small group: murals, group collages or constructions, illustrating a class book. Small group time can be the time to work together toward these ends. Some music and movement activities are more easily done in a small group of children. Listening skills are sharper and more focused (especially if you are in a separate location from the rest of the group). When using rhythm instruments, the volume is not as loud as in the large group. In movement activities, there are fewer bodies to fill the space and more room for each child to move freely.

Communicating with Others about Learning Standards

11

"All they do is play in that program." As early educators have continued to advocate for play-based curriculum, they have heard comments just like this. Parents and family members, administrators, community members, and policy makers do not necessarily understand the imbedding of learning and the attention to standards and goals for children in good early childhood practices. In fact, when I was teaching kindergarten, one of the parents of my students made a comment to me that stopped me in my tracks. She said:

> I can see that the children are immersed in reading and writing opportunities in this classroom. I can see that they are having fun and are very invested in what they are doing. My son loves coming to school. My problem is that I never see you teaching. Just what are you doing for these children?

I really had to step back and take a pause after this comment. Her words made me seriously rethink how I was communicating with others about the teaching approaches, curriculum planning, and assessment processes I was using.

I realized that this parent's concerns were not *her* problem—but *mine*. I had not clearly communicated to her what I was doing as I provided numerous opportunities for children to explore reading and writing with my friendly support and guidance. She identified teaching as instructing only. My methods looked unplanned and haphazard to her. I had not shared with her exactly what I was learning about her son's progress toward clear expectations in the area of literacy in a way that was meaningful to her.

I knew I was addressing early learning standards in my work, but others did not see it as clearly as I did. I had to make more evident and more public the work I was doing with the children and the ways in which I was measuring their progress and achievements. Beverly Falk (2000, 124) states:

> By *consciously* building standards into curriculum plans and assessment tasks and by *explicitly* gathering evidence of how standards are met, teachers, students, and their families gain a clear sense of what students know and can do. They get to see how students are progressing in relation to the standards, to other students, and more importantly, to themselves." (emphasis added)

There are key words in the quote above that help us remember how much we must make our attention to standards evident to others. By "consciously" identifying standards in our lesson and activity plans, in our daily routines, and as we see them in the play and exploration of young children, we will help others see how standards are interwoven in all that we do with the children. And by "explicitly gathering evidence of how standards are met," we will be able to show others just what we are seeing when children demonstrate for us the progress they are making toward specific learning goals. We have to provide "windows on learning" to those who do not see children's development in action as clearly as we do (Harris Helm, Beneke, Steinheimer 1998).

Communication Ideas

There are several ways to communicate to others how learning standards are coming alive in preschool programs. We can communicate through

- philosophy and mission statements;
- parent orientation materials and handouts;
- newsletters and announcements;
- postings of photos of children at work and play and children's work samples on parent and community bulletin boards;
- portfolios of observations of the children at work and play, including photos and work samples, and explanations of the standards involved.

Philosophy and Mission Statements

As a part of best practices, early childhood programs should have a statement of philosophy or a mission statement that is reflective of the beliefs and ideals to which all members of the organization strive. Such a statement helps teachers, directors, and families relate the everyday happenings in the program to an overarching set of goals and beliefs. Including information about your state's early learning standards and the way in which you are addressing those in your curriculum planning and assessment processes will make others aware of your efforts to work with the expectations set out by your state.

Here is an example of a mission and philosophy statement from a program that is accredited by NAEYC:

> "Our curriculum is based on the interests and needs of the children, providing developmentally appropriate practices for each age group and adapting to the needs of individual children. We embrace the philosophy that children learn best when they are actively involved in play, and when they have the opportunity to thoroughly explore, question, investigate, and manipulate objects and materials in their environment. Our teacher facilitated play-based learning provides children the opportunity to work and play with other children, to express themselves creatively through art, music, dramatic play and language, to communicate feelings and ideas, and to develop physical skills. The emphasis is on the Process not the Product—it is in the 'experience' that the foundation of learning is established. Throughout all that we do with children, we incorporate the goals of our state's early learning standards. We know there are recommended expectations for children's growth and development at various ages. We try to help each child achieve the expectations at a pace that is just right for that child. We use an assessment tool called *Focused Portfolios* to document and evaluate each child's development. Our educators will carefully observe each child as she plays, works, interacts, and goes about her daily routines at our program. These observations will be documented and tied to specific developmental milestones that we have identified to be important ones to help us see how each child is learning and growing in their days here.

The portfolios will be shared with parents at private conferences lasting twenty minutes that are scheduled in January. School will be closed during that time and childcare will be provided during the conference time." (Epworth Weekday Children's Ministry's *Parent Brochure and Handbook* 2005)

Parent Orientation Materials

Your philosophy and mission statement can be printed in brochures that are given to families interested in your program. And it can be included in parent orientation materials and handouts. In the program cited above, parents receive this information in many ways: in their parent handbooks, in informational sessions at the beginning of the school year, and again in a letter from the teachers in their first parent-teacher meeting. In addition, teachers use the above as talking points when they make their first contact with families and when they hold their first parent introductory sessions. This clear communication about incorporating standards in a play-based curriculum helps parents become more open to seeing this process in action. The conversation can change and grow, then, between teacher and parent to include a discussion of the goals for each child.

Newsletters and Announcements

Newsletters, announcements, and parent bulletin boards can also provide windows on learning and evidence of the way standards are addressed with the children. One teacher always used children's writing as the border for her newsletters for families. Another highlighted children's work in her newsletters and gave a brief explanation of what she saw in that work. She might have an artist of the week or include a writing sample. "Look how Juwan is learning to write his name!" Even though many of Juwan's letters were not accurately formed and a few were backward, she communicated enthusiastic acceptance that he was progressing just according to reasonable expectations for his age. By sharing many different levels of children's writing, parents got a clearer notion of the variability children show when working toward writing standards.

Telling stories about activities done in the classroom and relating those to what you are learning about the children's accomplishments can also be included in a newsletter. Sharing your lesson and activity plans with parents and highlighting the goals you have related to your plans will help them see how you are continually incorporating standards in all that you do. The Focused Early Learning Planning Framework shown in chapter 2 can be one way to clearly show how you are addressing standards and goals. One teacher who uses this framework stated: "The Focused Early Learning Frameworks state everything that I'm doing and show how I'm incorporating the Illinois Early Learning Standards throughout all of my activities" (Gronlund 2003, 128).

No matter what planning format you use, you can write the goals for activities on your plans rather than listing the materials you will use. In this way, you will keep standards much more at the focus for yourself and your colleagues. And you can post your plans or share them with families through your newsletters so that they can see the goals you are working on as well.

Bulletin Boards

Posting children's creations on parent bulletin boards and in hallways and public spaces provides another window on learning. Including a description of what the child was doing with the materials, and identifying the standards involved, can help others see that children demonstrate their learning in many different ways. Here is a photo of a teacher with children that was posted on a parent bulletin board with an explanation of the learning that was imbedded in that activity.

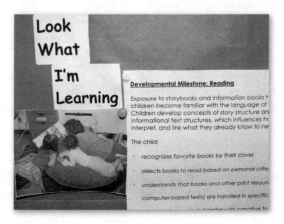

A documentation panel with photos and descriptions of children's block play can show how the children were matching shapes and building symmetrical towers, were cooperating and working together toward an end, and were devoting their attention and energies to staying with a task for a long period of time. All of these actions were building the foundational skills for becoming a lifelong learner! Documenting children's thinking around a group project or a thematic study can provide insight into their intellectual processes and language usage, expanding vocabulary, ability to make predictions and to follow through on experimentation, and hypothesis testing. You can find excellent ideas on creating effective documentation panels and displays in *Windows on Learning: Documenting Young Children's Work* (Harris Helm, Beneke, and Steinheimer 1998).

Portfolios

Anytime you are sharing photographs of children in action, you must make sure that you have parent permission to do so. Most parents will readily agree. But we must respect those who decline to give permission. In that case, a portfolio for the family's eyes alone can become a way to share the child's progress toward standards. As discussed in chapter 3, a portfolio that includes observations of the child's use of materials and interactions with others, as well as some photos and work samples, can be a powerful way to make standards come alive. As you invite parents to look at this collection of evidence and provide them with your evaluation of the child's skills and capabilities, you may hear comments like the following: "So, when you see him playing with these manipulative toys, you see his math skills developing? I didn't realize that. I thought he was just playing." You are educating others whenever you can clearly represent for them how you see standards in action in play and daily routines.

There are many ways to communicate how standards come alive in your early childhood program. You can embrace a child-centered, play-based curriculum and still imbed standards in all that you do. But you must make the ways you are addressing standards evident to others by providing as many windows on learning as you can!

References

Epworth Weekday Children's Ministry. 2005. *Parent brochure and handbook.* Indianapolis, IN: Epworth Methodist Church.

Falk, Beverly. 2000. *The heart of the matter: Using standards and assessment to learn.* Portsmouth, NH: Heinemann.

Gronlund, Gaye. 2003. *Focused early learning: A planning framework for teaching young children.* St. Paul: Redleaf.

Gronlund, Gaye, and Bev Engel. 2002. *Focused portfolios: A complete assessment for the young child.* St. Paul: Redleaf.

Harris Helm, Judy, Sallee Beneke, and Kathy Steinheimer. 1998. *Windows on learning: Documenting young children's work.* New York: Teachers College Press.

Improving Child Outcomes Related to Learning Standards While Advocating for Young Children

12

The development of early learning standards across the U.S. goes along with the desire to improve both short-term and long-term outcomes for young children. As the number of states providing preschool programs to children increases, the need for accountability about the benefits of these

programs and the spending of taxpayer dollars to support them will become even greater. There is already much research evidence that shows that preschool programs increase children's school readiness in the short term, and improve graduation rates, increase adult earnings, and lower crime rates in the long term (Shore, Bodrova, and Leong 2004). Now the questions are focusing on how we use early learning standards in appropriate ways that benefit children and help them reach their full potential. How do we help them develop as learners of the foundational skills that will serve them well as they move on to the elementary grades? And how do we track the improved outcomes for large groups of children across the country without resorting to inappropriate testing and teaching?

These are critical questions in the field of early childhood education at this time. It is tempting to take the easy way out: to push higher-grade-level curricular expectations and teaching approaches down to preschool and to collect information on children's progress that is more testlike in nature. Why is this easier? There are several reasons:

1. **Push-down curriculum immediately silences critics.** "Look. We've made the work harder. We have higher expectations. Our teaching approaches are more instructive in nature and the children look more like students in older grades, sitting and listening and doing lots of paper and pencil tasks. It's easy for others to see how we are

educating children when our teaching matches their perception of what a teacher does."

2. **Play looks like too much fun to others.** They don't see the learning and development of skills and concepts that is imbedded in it. And it's hard to communicate clearly about how standards are addressed in play and exploration to those who question such approaches. It takes time and effort to write out clear philosophy and mission statements, to educate parents and community members, to document and publicize children's learning through projects, learning areas and exploratory activities, and to put together portfolios that track children's progress tied to standards.

3. **Policy makers, administrators, and funding agencies often want quantitative data to show how children are progressing.** Quantitative data is easier to aggregate. It can be analyzed to show trends across large groups of children. It can be represented in graphs and tables and may be deemed "scientific" and therefore more reliable and valid by some policy makers (even though assessment experts question the reliability and validity of any testing of young children).

4. **In contrast, it is difficult to aggregate and gather information from authentic assessment measures for large groups of children.** It is labor-intensive, expensive, and time-consuming. Because authentic assessment is a more human endeavor, using teacher observations as the basis for gathering evidence and documentation about a child's progress is not seen as "scientific." Its reliability and validity is questioned because of potential teacher bias or flaws in the data collection and analysis involved.

Yet, as early educators who are committed to doing what's right for young children, we know that pushing children harder and using inappropriate teaching and assessment methods will not bring about long-term positive results for children. Instead using developmentally appropriate practices, imbedding standards in play and exploration, and using ongoing authentic assessment to track children's progress toward those standards are recommended.

How to Show Child Outcomes in Appropriate Ways

Some of the states in the U.S. are requiring that children's progress on early learning be recorded and monitored. And some are attempting to collect and analyze data about the performance of large groups of children related to early learning standards and still maintain a commitment to the best practices for young children.

California

In California, all programs are required to use the Desired Results Developmental Profile to track each child's developmental progress over time. Then, when the program goes through a Coordinated Compliance Review or a Contract Monitoring Review, staff members must be able to demonstrate that the findings on the profiles about children are being used to plan curriculum for the children (www.cde.ca.gov/sp/cd/ci/drdpinstructions.asp). In this way, California's standards must come alive in its early childhood programs! Others must be able to see how they are incorporated into planning and activities. This clearly places the responsibility on the shoulders of the early educators, rather than on the performance of the children on a test or one-time assessment.

Vermont

In Vermont, state-funded preschool programs for at-risk learners are asked to use assessment tools that align with the Vermont Early Learning Standards. Results of the children's performance are reported back to the state as a tally of the total number of indicators for each proficiency level across eight domains. Results are then aggregated for all of the children involved. The Vermont Early Education Initiative 2004-05 Year End Report states that "the developmental progress made by children was dramatic" (Squires 2005, 8).

James H. Squires, PhD, early childhood programs coordinator for the Vermont Department of Education, reports that the results are used to plan professional development, to look at the effectiveness of curriculum, and to report to the state board of education, commissioner, governor's office, and appropriate legislative committees.

Kentucky

Because of the newness of the Kentucky Early Childhood Standards, there are no requirements for programs to report outcomes related to children's achievement of the standards at this time. Instead, trainings are being conducted in the various recommended assessment tools and processes across the state. Kim Townley in the Early Childhood Development office of the Kentucky Department of Education reports that once these trainings are complete and people have developed competence and understanding in using the recommended assessments, they may be asked to report results of those assessments to the state.

New Mexico

This author is most familiar with an ongoing research project related to early learning standards in the state of New Mexico. There, the Office of Child Development in the Department of Children, Youth and Families launched a research project in July 2000. The goal of this project was to train early educators in state-funded child care programs in an authentic assessment method (specifically, Focused Portfolios) and to gather quantitative data about child outcomes as well. The overriding philosophy of the project was "Do no harm to children or families." Therefore, any form of testing or one-time assessment was not to be included. Instead, teacher observations of children's performance related to specific early learning standards were collected and teachers were trained to write factual, detailed observations of the children's performance for these specific standards. Then these observations were coded and rated numerically so that they could be analyzed statistically. As of September 2005, this project entered its sixth year with more than 13,600 observations on 1,660 children submitted by 256 teachers from thirty-two programs across the state of New Mexico.

Each year, these observations were analyzed in order to determine the progress seen in the child's performance from a fall observation to one in the spring. Such progress might involve moving from a lower-level standard to a higher one. Or such progress might be seen by smaller steps the child took in working toward accomplishment of a standard. In order to capture these smaller steps toward progress, five-point rubric scales were developed for each standard. Independent judges read through the observations and scored them by identifying a standard and assigning a rubric rating.

Throughout the years of the project, a clear majority of the samples have documented progress for children's performance in regard to the standards identified. One New Mexico official cited this study as "the gold standard of research." For more details about this study, you can contact me or the Office of Child Development in Santa Fe, New Mexico (see contact information at the end of this chapter).

It is important to use early learning standards to benefit children. As the models reported above demonstrate, outcomes can be measured in such a way that children are asked to demonstrate their work toward standards through their performance on authentic, meaningful tasks. And ways to quantify and aggregate the results are being used and developed in states across the nation. In these ways, early educators can stay true to best practices and integrate early learning standards into curriculum and assessment that is just right for young children.

References

California Department of Education. 2005. Desired results developmental profile instructions. www.cde.ca.gov/sp/cd/ci/drdpinstructions.asp.

Shore, Rima, Elena Bodrova, and Deborah Leong. 2004. Child outcome standards in pre-K programs: What are standards; what is needed to make them work? *Preschool Policy Matters* (National Institute for Early Education Research), no. 5.

Squires, James H. 2005. The Vermont early education initiative 2004-05 year end report. Vermont Department of Education.

Contact Information

Gaye Gronlund
Indianapolis, IN
(317) 823-8860
gayegronlund@yahoo.com

New Mexico Office of Child Development
Santa Fe, NM
(505) 827-7946

Rigorous Academics in Preschool and Kindergarten? Yes! Let Me Tell You How.

A swelling tide of media coverage places early childhood educators in a difficult position. This coverage takes the complex issues involved in planning curriculum for three-, four-, and five-year-olds and distills the debate into pablum preschools and kindergartens versus academically rigorous ones.

Many teachers of young children are demonstrating their courage and convictions by standing up to this oversimplification. They carefully explain developmentally appropriate practice to families in their programs, to administrators and community members, to school boards and funding organizations. With pride they announce, "I support learning for young children! Let me show you how that learning takes place in my preschool or kindergarten classroom."

High-quality early childhood programs across the country address academics, including assessment, and are accountable to early childhood standards. Research and professionally recommended practices recognize that young children learn best through manipulation of materials and hands-on experiences carefully planned and facilitated by knowledgeable teachers. This learning looks very much like play—but play with purpose and intent.

The teacher initially defines that purpose and intent, but only after following the children's interests. She sets up a learning environment that has inherent structure and stimulation for children. She organizes and displays materials so that children use them to figure things out, practice skills, and learn new concepts. Children are allowed enough time to explore those materials again and again, so that through repetition and success they develop the confidence to take risks and try new activities with more complexity and demands.

Most important, the teacher is ever ready to teach. However, that teaching may look quite different for each child and for each particular situation that arises during a day with young children.

Much of the misunderstanding in the debate between pablum preschools and kindergartens and academically rigorous ones stems from the definition of what it means to teach young children. Many people see a teacher only as an instructor, imparting concepts and skills to patiently listening young children. That instruction is teacher-directed; the children are passive receivers of the information that the teacher dispenses. The children demonstrate their understanding through paper-and-pencil tasks (usually workbooks or ditto sheets), and their progress is evaluated through on-demand assessments or tests.

Good early childhood practices acknowledge that three-, four-, and five-year-olds are wigglers and doers. To help children stay with tasks and learn important concepts and skills, teachers work with, instead of against, their individual developmental styles. The teacher's role then becomes one of observer as the child goes about exploring materials. He asks open-ended questions that stimulate the child's thinking: "What do you think would happen if you tried . . . ?" He helps promote vocabulary development by describing what the child is doing: "I see you've used lots of colors—red, green, blue, and brown." He models or demonstrates how to make shapes with the geoboards or count all of the big blocks. He illustrates how to crack open an egg or how much food to feed the fish.

Teachers of preschool and kindergarten are rigorously academic because they keep goals in mind as they continually interact with children in their play and exploration. To develop reading and writing skills, teachers read many stories each day to and with children. Through these reading experiences,

children learn many of the conventions of written language, including left to right and top to bottom directionality; use picture clues; make logical predictions; and play with the sounds of language. Teachers help children learn to recognize their own names and encourage the writing of names and other words as children demonstrate interest. They provide a variety of alphabet activities and offer opportunities to act out familiar stories and draw and write daily. To meet the goals of developing young children as readers and writers, teachers embed literacy activities in meaningful experiences: writing letters to friends, reading the classroom helper chart, and labeling the classroom. They read favorite books again and again so that familiarity becomes a form of practice and more and more awareness of print is developed.

Preschool and kindergarten teachers pay close attention to academics when they also embed math, science, and social studies activities in children's exploration and purposeful play. Counting and one-to-one correspondence are evident in daily routines of attendance and setting the table for snack. Geometry is explored in block building and use of many other manipulatives. Vocabulary and an understanding of measurement are taught at the sand and water table or in cooking activities. Scientific study and observation is developed in early childhood classrooms through projects and units of study about weather, seasonal changes, and plant and animal life. Social studies concepts of community and family life and the study of people and their differences and similarities are included in dramatic play, literature, and cultural celebrations.

What are not evident in high-quality preschool and kindergarten classrooms are skill-and-drill activities. Instead, the learning of all academic subjects is playful and exploratory. Children contribute their own ideas, use their own problem-solving strategies, and pursue their own interests. Teachers skillfully weave in the goals and objectives of traditional academics as they build on what children can do and challenge them to try new things. Children are not left to their own devices, nor is their development left to chance. Using classroom-based assessment practices such as careful observation and anecdotal documentation, as well as collecting children's work (taking photographs or samples of children's drawings, writing, and language), teachers continually evaluate the progress the children are making. This ongoing assessment process provides more reliable information than tests or on-demand tasks; teachers are accountable for what each child knows and can do, and they use that to make decisions on how best to teach each child.

Most teachers recognize that we must have expectations and standards for our early childhood programs. But they also know the nature of learning at this age, and they carefully define how academics are most appropriately and effectively incorporated into preschool and kindergarten programs. Because a program uses playful ways to build children's success does not mean the curriculum is not rigorous or academic. It means that it is just right for what's best for three-, four-, and five-year-old children.

This article by Gaye Gronlund first appeared in *Young Children* (NAEYC) 56, no. 2 (2001): 42–45.

Terms Related to Early Learning Standards

Types of Standards

The following definitions are taken from Shore, Rima, Elena Bodrova, and Deborah Leong. 2004. Child outcome standards in pre-K programs: What are standards; what is needed to make them work? *Preschool Policy Matters* (National Institute for Early Education Research), no. 5.

Program Standards—The resources, activities, and instruction that programs offer to help children learn (incorporates both Classroom Standards and Teaching and Curriculum Standards).

Classroom Standards—Identify classroom characteristics such as the maximum number of children in a classroom; the allowable ratio of adults to children; and the materials and supports available to children and families.

Teaching and Curriculum Standards—Sometimes described as opportunities to learn . . . educational experiences . . . or activities . . . generally intended to guide administrators.

Child Outcome Standards—Describe the knowledge and skills children should acquire by the end of the year (encompasses Content Standards and Performance Standards).

Content Standards—Define the range of knowledge and skills that children should master.

Performance Standards—Describe how it can be demonstrated that children have met the content standards.

Assessment

The following definitions are taken from Early Childhood Education Assessment Consortium, Council of Chief State School Officers. The words we use: A glossary of terms for early childhood education standards and assessment. www.ccsso.org/projects/SCASS/Projects/Early_Childhood_Education_Assessment_Consortium/publications_and_products/2840.cfm)

Benchmarks—Clear, specific descriptions of knowledge or skill that can be supported through observations, descriptions, and documentations of a child's performance or behavior and by samples of child's work often used as points of reference in connection with more broadly stated content standards. . . . *Benchmarks* are *performance standards* (e.g., data from previous years) against which other performances (e.g., data from the current year) are judged. *Performance standards* and *benchmarks* are similar to *indicators,* but different in that indicators typically are used to show either incline or decline in an item under study and are often expressed as a statistic. *Performance standards* or *benchmarks* usually express upward growth in a child's knowledge or skill.

Performance-Based (Alternate, Alternative, Authentic) Assessment—Any assessment strategy designed to estimate a child's knowledge, understanding, ability, skill, and/or attitudes in a consistent fashion across individuals emphasizing methods other than standardized achievement tests, particularly those using multiple choice formats. Performance-based assessments typically include exhibitions, investigations, demonstrations, written or oral responses, journals, and portfolios.

Observational Assessment—A process in which the teacher systematically observes and records information about the child's level of development and/or knowledge, skills, and attitudes in order to make a determination about what has been learned, improve teaching, and support children's progress. A checklist or notes are often used to record what has been observed.

Portfolio Assessment—A collection of work, usually drawn from children's classroom work, which, when subjected to objective analysis, become an assessment tool. This occurs when (1) the assessment purpose is defined; (2) criteria or methods are made clear for determining what is put into the portfolio, by whom, and when; and (3) criteria for assessing either the collection or individual pieces of work are identified and used to make judgments about children's learning.